Teaching Dante's
Divine Comedy

Approaches to Teaching
World Literature

Joseph Gibaldi, series editor

For a complete listing of titles,
see the last pages of this book.

Approaches to Teaching Dante's *Divine Comedy*

Edited by

Carole Slade

Consultant Editor

Giovanni Cecchetti

The Modern Language Association of
America   1982

© 1982 by The Modern Language Association of America
All rights reserved. Printed in the United States of America

Library of Congress Cataloging-in-Publication Data
Approaches to teaching Dante's Divine comedy.
  (Approaches to teaching masterpieces of world literature; 2)
  Bibliography: p.
  Includes index.
  Contents: Materials/Carole Slade—"An introduction
to Dante's Divine comedy"/Giovanni Cecchetti—
"Dante's Divine comedy"/Glauco Cambon—[etc.]
  1. Dante Alighieri, 1265–1321. Divina commedia—
Addresses, essays, lectures. 2. Dante Alighieri,   ③ Italian literature —
1265–1321—Study and teaching—Addresses, essays,   H & C.
lectures. I. Slade, Carole. II. Cecchetti,
Giovanni, 1922– . III. Series. IV. Divine comedy.
PQ4371.A6 Prof 851'.1   81–11251
ISBN 0–87352–477–2   AACR2
ISBN 0–87352–478–0 (pbk.)

Fourth printing 1996
Printed on recycled paper

Cover illustration of the paperback edition: Entrance into Purgatory,
from Purgatorio 9, MS. 514 (c. 1350), Library of the Earl of
Leicester, Holkham Hall, England

Published by The Modern Language Association of America
10 Astor Place, New York, New York 10003-6981

CONTENTS

PART TWO: APPROACHES

PREFACE TO THE SERIES

In his thoughtful and sensitive book *The Art of Teaching* (1950), Gilbert Highet wrote, "Bad teaching wastes a great deal of effort, and spoils many lives which might have been full of energy and happiness." All too many teachers have failed in their work, Highet argued, simply "because they have not thought about it." It is our hope that the Approaches to Teaching Masterpieces of World Literature series, sponsored by the Modern Language Association's Committee on Teaching and Related Professional Activities, will not only improve the craft—as well as the art—of teaching but also enhance in these years of a "publish and/or perish" mentality an awareness of the importance of teaching in our profession and encourage serious and continuing discussion of the aims and methods of our teaching.

The principal objective of the series is to collect within each volume a number of points of view on teaching a particular work of world literature that is widely taught at the undergraduate level. The preparation of each volume will begin with a survey of diverse philosophies of and approaches to teaching the work in question, thus enabling us to include in the volume the thoughts and methods of scores of teachers with considerable experience in teaching the work at the undergraduate level. The result will be a source book of material, information, and ideas on teaching the work to undergraduates.

The introductory portion of each volume will be devoted to a presentation and analysis of the information and issues emerging from the survey and will include a discussion of such matters as preferred editions, suggested background materials, useful teaching aids, and so on. In the remainder of the volume, a number of experienced teachers will discuss their particular approaches to the work.

We expect a wide-ranging audience for the series, for each of its volumes will be intended to serve both the inexperienced and the experienced teacher of a literary work at the undergraduate level, those who wish to learn new ways of teaching as well as those who wish to compare their own approaches with the approaches of colleagues in other schools. Of course, no volume in the series could ever serve as a substitute for erudition, intelligence, creativity, and sensitivity in teaching. We hope merely that each book will point readers in useful directions; at most each will offer only a first step in the long journey to successful teaching.

We live in a time that increasingly demands a rededication to under-graduate teaching of the humanities, a time, in fact, that presents us with almost daily struggles for the survival of the humanities and of the idea of a liberal education. It may well be that our sometimes divided and fragmented profession will rediscover in its concern for and com-mitment to teaching a sense of purpose, unity, and community that many believe it presently lacks.

We hope that the Approaches to Teaching Masterpieces of World Literature series will serve in some small way to refocus attention upon the importance of teaching and to improve undergraduate in-struction. We may perhaps adopt as keynote for the series Alfred North Whitehead's observation in *The Aims of Education* (1929) that the essence of a liberal education "proceeds by imparting a knowledge of the masterpieces of thought, of imaginative literature, and of art."

Joseph Gibaldi
Series Editor

PREFACE TO THE VOLUME

Poi quando fuor da noi tanto divise
quell'ombre, che veder più non potiersi,
novo pensiero dentro a me si mise,
del qual più altri nacquero e diversi;
e tanto d'uno in altro vaneggiai,
che li occhi per vaghezza ricopersi,
e 'l pensamento in signo trasmutai.

Then when those shades were so far parted from us that they could no more be seen, a new thought arose within me, from which others many and diverse were born; and I so rambled from one to another that, wandering thus, I closed my eyes, and transmuted my musing into a dream.

Purg. XVIII.139–45
trans. Charles S. Singleton

Here in the middle of his journey the pilgrim's thoughts of encounters with an overwhelming number of souls multiply into dizzying memories and dreams. The experience of confronting the souls in Dante's three realms through reading the *Divine Comedy* can prove equally intense as the rich detail and archetypal design awaken emotional and intellectual reactions. But the poem poses many obstacles to understanding that challenge our resourcefulness as teachers. We must devote many of our class sessions to the necessary biographical, historical, and theological background, while attempting to preserve the spontaneity of a first reading for students. And because many of us today do not share Dante's belief in the tenets of medieval Christianity and the inherent order of the universe governing the thought and shape of the poem, the seriousness with which Dante takes his mission to comprehend the totality of creation and to judge the society of his day needs careful presentation if it is not to seem naive rather than magnificent. In sum, teaching students to read the *Divine Comedy* entails working out with them new definitions of such basic concepts as order, justice, and love; their new perceptions demand not only new knowledge—attained comparatively easily—but also changes in attitude and outlook.

Some of the solutions to these and other problems related to teaching the *Divine Comedy* may be found in the works of the critics of Dante; other solutions must be discovered by each teacher in the classroom. The purpose of this volume is to help provide insight into both the critical materials and the teaching techniques that have proved effective for teaching Dante at the undergraduate level. Part I provides information to guide in the selection of a teaching edition of the *Divine Comedy* and secondary works for a reading list for both instructors and students. Part II presents essays by sixteen teachers on various methods of constructing courses and conducting classes on the *Divine Comedy*. These essays, largely personal in nature, represent a range of individual approaches and solutions. A bibliography of works cited and an index conclude the volume.

While this volume addresses itself primarily to beginning instructors and nonspecialists, we hope that scholars of Dante also will find here some applicable ideas about teaching the *Divine Comedy*. It is assumed that the teacher has had graduate training in one or more related fields, though perhaps not specifically in Dante studies, and that preparation for teaching the *Divine Comedy* will not only encompass the works mentioned here but range beyond them as well. The volume in no way replaces thorough study of Dante, but it does seek to confront the reality that persons with a wide variety of backgrounds find themselves teaching Dante, perhaps because of assignment to a course such as world literature or the creation of an interdisciplinary survey of the Middle Ages.

The nature of the audience has determined many characteristics of the volume. Discussions here deal exclusively with teaching the *Divine Comedy* to undergraduates and therefore treat issues involved in introducing the work rather than in presenting subtle points or specialized interpretations. Since the volume is directed toward those teaching in the United States, it concentrates on works readily available to students in American undergraduate colleges. Texts of the *Divine Comedy*, reference works, and introductory studies in Italian are included, but works in other languages have been omitted on the assumption that the experienced teacher will locate them in the bibliographies as the need arises. Highly specialized studies receive little mention, and limitations of space require an emphasis on book-length studies and the omission of pamphlets and articles. In all areas this work is introductory rather than exhaustive, suggestive rather than prescriptive, and descriptive rather than critical.

Preparation of the volume began in the fall of 1978, when the Modern Language Association sent questionnaires requesting a wide range of information to members of the profession who teach Dante. The response to the survey revealed that a volume of practical information on teaching would be welcomed by many teachers. Contributors to the volume were selected from the respondents to the questionnaire to represent a variety of viewpoints and teaching situations. This book reflects all of the questionnaires in some way, however, for together the responses provide a comprehensive picture of the teaching of Dante in colleges and universities around the country. Regardless of the challenges that the *Divine Comedy* presents, many teachers have their most successful and satisfying classroom experiences with the work. This volume attempts to share their discoveries.

I am pleased to acknowledge a great deal of assistance from many quarters. First, I wish to thank the participants in the Modern Language Association survey, whose responses provided the foundation and the stimulus for this work, and the members of the MLA Committee on Teaching and Related Professional Activities for their sponsorship of this series. Joseph Gibaldi, general editor of the series, provided experienced judgment on every issue; Giovanni Cecchetti, consultant editor of the volume, made sound improvements at several stages; and Thomas G. Bergin read and commented wisely and generously on the final draft.

I am grateful to the Faculty Development Committee and the Office of Research Administration at Baylor University for their generous support of work on this project. Robert G. Collmer, Clement Goode, Patricia Howard, Ann V. Miller, and other colleagues at Baylor contributed valuable insights. Mary Margaret Stewart, Pamela Hicks, Leesa Stroman, and Lisa Hutton provided very able assistance with typing and preparation of the manuscript.

For most important encouragement along the way I thank Jeffrey Slade.

CS

Part One

MATERIALS

Carole Slade

EDITIONS

This section surveys many of the available editions and translations of the *Divine Comedy*. All texts presented below appear in Works Cited under the name of the translator or, when the translation appears in an anthology or collection, of the editor.

Italian Editions

No definitive text of the *Divine Comedy* exists, since a holograph copy has not been found. Even early manuscripts differ considerably. Scholars in the nineteenth and twentieth centuries have established texts through various procedures, but differences of opinion remain. The most recent text, *La commedia secondo l'antica vulgata* (1966–67), was commissioned by the Società Dantesca Italiana and supervised by Giorgio Petrocchi. This new edition, hailed as a significant stride toward an authoritative text, consists of four volumes, with the first devoted to an introduction concerning in part the philological research undertaken for the reconstruction of the manuscript tradition. Harvard University Press adopted the Petrocchi text for a one-volume edition with notes and apparatus from Charles H. Grandgent's widely used text (1909; 2nd rev. ed., 1933). Charles S. Singleton has updated the text, adjusted the commentary to account for recent scholarship, and added notes on archaic Italian forms and Latin passages. The notes and introductory summaries in English and the one-volume format with generous spacing make it convenient for the undergraduate classroom.

The prior text of the Società Dantesca Italiana, *Testo critico della divina commedia*, by Giuseppe Vandelli, remains important, and several editions of it are popular with American teachers. The edition by Natalino Sapegno (1955; rev. ed., 1968), which follows the Vandelli text while taking the Petrocchi text into account in the revised edition, receives praise for the extensive notes and commentary. Sapegno paraphrases difficult passages and provides explanatory materials on all aspects of the work, including parallels to Dante's other works and mention of his sources. The Vandelli text is also available with the commentary by Tommaso Casini (1902), as revised by S. A. Barbi (1921). This commentary, originally intended for students as well as scholars, remains a favorite for classroom use because of the clear, complete notes providing cross-references, explications, and critical opinions.

3

Translations: Dual-Language Editions and English Editions

Traduttore traditore ("the translator is a traitor"). Nearly every translator of Dante has recognized the truth of this Italian proverb in a humble acknowledgment of the extraordinary difficulty of doing justice to Dante, labeled by Byron "the most untranslatable of poets." In seeking to preserve certain aspects of Dante's poetry, each translator acknowledges that other facets of Dante will be lost in translation. Most translators would likely agree with Dorothy Sayers that the highest compliment their translation could receive would be that it compelled readers to turn to Dante in the original Italian.

Teachers generally expect a translation to convey the feeling and sense of the original, and in the case of the *Divine Comedy* opinion divides sharply over whether a prose or a verse translation best achieves this goal. Translators themselves have wrestled with the choice, some ardently advocating one form or another. Most commentators agree, however, that both forms have advantages. A prose translation perhaps best communicates the literal meaning, whereas a translation in verse gives a feeling for the movement and rhythm of Dante's poetry. The immense number of rhymes required by Dante's terza rima (*aba, bcb, cdc,* etc.) presents a problem in English, however, and some translators in verse reduce the demand by leaving out the linking rhyme to create a form called defective or "dummy" terza rima, while others eliminate rhyme entirely, using blank verse or another unrhymed form.

Teachers can choose from a number of fine translations of the *Divine Comedy*. The listing here presents those most often used in the undergraduate classroom. Many instructors make more than one translation available to students, for no single translation presents all of Dante.

To provide an initial impression of the method and style of the translations, a quotation of three lines (*Inf.* XII.1–3) appears after each discussion. The passage selected presents a number of difficulties to a translator, as the Italian original and my own literal prose translation below demonstrate:

> Era lo loco, ov' a scender la riva
> venimmo, alpestro e, per quel ch'iv'er' anco
> tal ch'ogne vista ne sarebbe schiva.

The place, where we came to down the bank, was mountainous, and because of what was there, such that every eye would avoid it.

(*Inf.* XII.1–3)

The inversion of subject and verb in line 1, with the consequent problem of the placement of the modifying clause, and the euphemistic circumlocution in lines 2 and 3 make the choice of both syntax and diction problematic in English.

The translations of the *Divine Comedy* discussed below appear in two basic formats: dual-language editions and English editions. These works are available in paperbound editions.

Some teachers believe that all students, even those who do not know Italian, should have the original text before them as they read. In fact, T. S. Eliot and others have claimed that they learned to read Italian by referring back and forth to an English translation of the *Divine Comedy*. A number of texts provide a dual-language format.

A popular edition is John D. Sinclair's well-respected prose translation (*Inferno*, 1939; *Purgatorio*, 1939; *Paradiso*, 1946). Sinclair chose prose to achieve his goal of "combining a close rendering of the Italian with the requirements of a credible English. . . ." The translation, which has been praised as accurate and readable, though some find it slightly outdated and flat, faces the Vandelli text. Explanatory notes, described by one instructor as "jewel-like," summarize the action of each canto and treat historical background, aesthetic qualities, and critical attitudes. The brief endnotes are designated by number in the translation, and each volume contains an outline of the "system" of the realm.

> The place where we came for the descent of the steep was alpine, and besides, because of what was there, a place every eye would shun.
>
> trans. John D. Sinclair

Charles S. Singleton's dual-language edition of the *Divine Comedy* in the Bollingen Series provides an extremely clear and accurate translation. Each canticle was originally published individually in a two-volume, clothbound format (*Inferno*, 1970; *Purgatorio*, 1973; *Paradiso*, 1975). The first volume of each contains the text and translation. The prose, set in narrow columns to correspond to the facing Italian, allows the reader to follow the narrative rapidly or to use the English version as an aid to comprehending the original. The extensive commentary in the accompanying volume provides materials such as quotations from Dante's sources (both in the original language and in English), parallels in such areas as theology and mythology, and analyses of textual, linguistic, historical, and biographical issues. Summaries of the cantos are not included, and rather than providing lengthy explanations in any one place, Singleton allows for "gradual revelation of meaning" throughout a reading of the entire work. The price of the hardcover edition has prevented most instructors from using the Singleton translation, though many have said they would like to. Fortunately, Princeton University Press has published a one-volume paperbound edition of the text, translation, and commentary of the *Inferno*.

> The place where we came for the descent of the bank was alpine, and such, because of what was there, that every eye would shun it.
>
> trans. Charles S. Singleton

The MLA survey of teachers of Dante indicated that the most widely used translations in the American undergraduate classroom at present are those of John Ciardi, Dorothy Sayers, and Mark Musa.

John Ciardi's "verse rendering for the modern reader" (*Inferno*, 1954; *Purgatorio*, 1961; *Paradiso*, 1970) has been both popular and controversial. Ciardi chose "dummy" or defective terza rima in order to use idiomatic English while communicating the feel of the poem. At the end of each canto he adds a rhyming couplet not found in the original. Ciardi's translation has been praised as vivid, forceful, and natural, and many teachers find that it generates excitement in the classroom. Some believe that the translation is not entirely scholarly, however, and that unjustifiable liberties have been taken with the text. The canticles appear in separate volumes, the *Inferno* and *Purgatorio* with historical introductions by Archibald T. MacAllister, and the *Paradiso* with an introduction by John Freccero. A brief summary precedes each canto, and notes designated by line follow the entire canto. The notes, which deal with literary, linguistic, historical, and theological matters, have been described as complete and clear. Several illustrations accompany each volume.

> The scene that opened from the edge of the pit
> was mountainous, and such a desolation
> that every eye would shun the sight of it:
>
> trans. John Ciardi

Dorothy Sayers' translation (*Inferno*, 1949; *Purgatorio*, 1955; *Paradiso*, completed by Barbara Reynolds, 1962), a widely read version, appears in the Penguin Classics series. In her introduction to the *Inferno* Sayers acknowledges the difficulties of terza rima, but defends it as the only way to capture the speed, rhythm, and punch of Dante's verse. The strengths of the translation are its vigor and inventive use of rhyme, but some criticize the mixture of levels of diction and what they consider idiosyncrasies. Most critics concur that Sayers and Reynolds' *Paradiso* is the strongest of the three canticles in this translation. Each volume contains a substantial introduction by Sayers, numerous charts and diagrams, appendixes, a cross-referenced glossary, and a bibliography. A short summary precedes each canto, while explanatory notes indicated by line number follow. A writer of fiction, Sayers emphasizes the narrative qualities of the *Divine Comedy* in her commentaries.

> The place we came to, to descend the brink from,
> Was sheer crag; and there was a Thing there—making
> All told, a prospect any eye would shrink from.
> trans. Dorothy Sayers

Mark Musa's translation of the *Inferno* is frequently used in college classrooms, particularly in the format as a selection in the *Norton Anthology of World Masterpieces* (4th ed., 1980), edited by Maynard Mack. In his introduction Musa writes that he selected unrhymed iambic pentameter as the best means of reaching his goal of a simple and accurate translation. Many have praised his work as faithful and scholarly, while others have disagreed with his interpretations of certain passages. In the Indiana University volume, one-paragraph summaries of all thirty-four cantos precede the entire text, and endnotes indicated by line number provide summaries of critical opinions, disputed points, historical background, and Musa's own readings. Pen-and-ink drawings by Richard M. Powers illustrate the volume.

> Not only was that place, where we had come
> to descend, craggy, but there was something there
> that made the scene appalling to the eye.
> trans. Mark Musa

The complete *Divine Comedy* is available in several one-volume paperbound editions that some instructors find convenient. Thomas G. Bergin, a prominent scholar and critic, prepared his translation (*In-

ferno, 1948; *Purgatorio,* 1953; *Paradiso,* 1954) for the Crofts Classics series, which limits volumes to 128 pages. The edition uses small type, abbreviated notes, and the presentation of several cantos in summary form to make a compact edition. The format, however, has perhaps deflected attention from the translation, which has been praised as accurate and scholarly. Bergin writes in his introduction that he chose blank verse (with several rhymed passages) to achieve "readability." He has lengthened, condensed, and transposed lines to gain clarity, but some critics have objected to his alterations of Dante's lines. The volume includes a short introduction to the *Divine Comedy,* "Notes on Italian Pronunciation," "The Principal Dates in Dante's Life," plans of the three realms, an excerpt from the *Cronica* of Giovanni Villani, a list of celestial orders, a short bibliography, and notes at the foot of each page.

> Where our descent began the craggy path
> Was steep and barred by such a monstrous sight
> As travelers would tremble to confront.
> > trans. Thomas G. Bergin

The translation by Laurence Binyon, British poet and art historian (*Inferno,* 1933; *Purgatorio,* 1938; *Paradiso,* 1943), is available in a Viking Portable Library volume edited by Paolo Milano and in the Random House anthology *Western Literature II,* edited by Robert Hollander and A. Bartlett Giamatti. Ezra Pound reviewed Binyon's *Inferno* rather favorably and made suggestions for Binyon's *Purgatorio.* The Binyon version in terza rima has been commended for accuracy and criticized for a lack of poetic intensity. The language now seems somewhat antiquated and the syntax strained. A short summary of the action precedes each canto, and short notes appear at the bottom of each page. The volume also contains other works by Dante: the complete *Vita nuova* translated by Dante Gabriel Rossetti, as well as nine of the *Rime* and short excerpts from *De Vulgari Eloquentia, De Monarchia,* and the *Epistles.* Milano's introduction, in which T. S. Eliot's perceptions figure importantly, covers Dante's life and the nature of the *Divine Comedy.*

> Craggy the place was where for our advance
> We must descend, and by such presence marred,
> That any eye would look on it askance.
> > trans. Laurence Binyon

H. R. Huse's prose translation of the complete *Divine Comedy* (1954) comes in a Rinehart edition. Huse's prose is spaced and printed like the original tercet form to preserve the "unity of thought" of the original tercet. This translation has been characterized as direct and faithful, if somewhat flat, but some have pointed out inaccuracies. The volume has unique typographical features: short summaries inserted throughout each canto to eliminate page turning and bracketed explanations of elements such as names and pronouns within the text. Footnotes are brief, and the text ends with a glossary. The volume includes an introduction by Huse, as well as diagrams and charts of the canticles.

> The place where we came to descend the bank
>> was craggy and, because of what was there [the Minotaur],
>> such that every eye would shun it.
>>>> trans. H. R. Huse

Louis Biancolli's translation of the *Divine Comedy* (1969) in blank verse, while not widely used by teachers, received praise from several respondents to the MLA survey. This version in "flexible iambic pentameter" has the advantage or disadvantage, depending on the point of view, of appearing without notes, with the exception of translations for Latin passages.

> The place to which we came for climbing down
> The bank looked alpine, and what was there, moreover,
> Would have turned every eye away in horror.
>>>> trans. Louis Biancolli

Some instructors continue to use an old translation in prose known as the Carlyle-Okey-Wicksteed translation. John Aitken Carlyle's *Inferno* (1849), Thomas Okey's *Purgatorio* (1901), and Philip Henry Wicksteed's *Paradiso* (1899) are published in a one-volume Vintage edition. The translation of the *Purgatorio*, notes by Hermann Oelsner, and arguments by Wicksteed are considered the strong points of this work, which remains very readable.

> The place to which we came, in order to descend the bank, was alpine, and such, from what was there besides, that every eye would shun it.
>>>> trans. John Aitken Carlyle

The study of Dante provides a good opportunity to talk about the process of translation. Nearly every translator prefaces the work with a statement on the subject, and the remarks of Bergin, Ciardi, Musa, and Sayers are particularly informative. In addition, the following books provide useful analyses of specific translations and problems peculiar to translating Dante. In his two-volume study *The* Divine Comedy *in English: A Critical Bibliography* (1965–67) Gilbert F. Cunningham devotes a chapter to each translator of the *Divine Comedy* into English through 1967, beginning with the first English version by Charles Rogers in 1782. Cunningham discusses relevant biographical information, offers an analysis and evaluation of each translation with examples, and outlines the critical reception of the translation. William J. DeSua's *Dante into English: A Study of the Translation of the* Divine Comedy *in Britain and America* (1964) relates attitudes toward Dante in various periods to the quantity and quality of translations, in chapters entitled "The Renovators: Dante's Eighteenth Century British Translators," "The Reflectors: Dante's Romantic Translators," "The Literalists: Dante's Victorian Translators," and "Craftsmen and Critics: Dante's Twentieth Century Translators." The work also assesses selected translations and contains a chronological list of translations.

REFERENCE WORKS

Numerous reference works exist to aid the study of the *Divine Comedy*—encyclopedias, dictionaries, concordances, and bibliographies—and most of them can assist not only the scholar but also the beginning student of Dante. A library supporting serious study of the *Divine Comedy* should contain many, if not all, of these.

The recent five-volume *Enciclopedia dantesca* (1970–76), directed by Umberto Bosco and edited by Giorgio Petrocchi and others, is a monumental work. Covering the complete works, entries include Dante's Italian words with a listing of each appearance and discussion of meanings, foreign words within Italian works, Latin words with cultural or doctrinal significance, all proper nouns, the fortune of Dante's poem in numerous countries, and profiles of prominent Dante scholars. Appendixes include one on Dante's syntax and another on his life. A brief bibliography follows the entries, which are signed. Citations from the *Divine Comedy* refer to Petrocchi's edition, with additional reference to previous editions. This encyclopedia is a necessity for advanced study of Dante. No comparable work exists in English. An earlier Italian encyclopedia that remains of interest is G. A. Scartazzini's *Enciclopedia dantesca: Dizionario critico e ragionato di quanto concerne la vita e le opere di Dante Alighieri* (1896–1905).

Paget Toynbee's classic work *A Dictionary of Proper Names and Notable Matters in the Works of Dante* (1898), revised and updated by Charles S. Singleton in 1968, continues to be the most valuable dictionary in English. The volume includes tables, plates, maps, and bibliography, along with listings of names, places, and concepts in Dante's works. Toynbee frequently uses direct quotation from texts such as Dante's sources and early commentaries. An abridged version, *Concise Dictionary of Proper Names and Notable Matters in the Works of Dante* (1914), is also currently in print. A dictionary in Italian that is comprehensive and authoritative while compact is Giorgio Siebzehner-Vivanti's *Dizionario della* Divina commedia (1954), which is available in paperbound form.

The most recent concordance in English, *A Concordance to the* Divine Comedy, published by the Dante Society of America, refers to the Vandelli text. The purpose of the work as stated in the introduction is "to enable the user to locate readily any passage he desires, to provide groupings of references useful for the study of any particular phase of Dante's thought, and, finally, to provide a conspectus of the significant words and forms of the poet's vocabulary." Latin words are treated in an appendix. Edward Allen Fay's *Concordance of the* Divina commedia (1888), which is based on Karl Witte's 1862 edition, now has only limited usefulness. A work in Italian, *Concordanza della* Commedia *di Dante Alighieri* (1975), edited by Luciano Lovera, uses the new Petrocchi text.

The best sources of current bibliography on Dante are those periodicals that devote either entire issues or permanent sections to current work on Dante. In the United States the most complete of these is *Dante Studies with the Annual Report of the Dante Society* (before 1966, *Annual Report of the Dante Society*). The "American Dante Bibliography," compiled since 1957 by Anthony L. Pellegrini, editor of the journal, provides an annotated listing of translations, books, articles, editions, studies, dissertations, and reviews published in the United States, as well as foreign reviews of American studies. Entries are alphabetized by author, and a section of addenda covers works published in other years but not previously noted. This bibliography is indispensable for the American student and teacher of Dante.

The *MLA International Bibliography*, a listing of books and articles published in the United States and abroad, includes under the general heading "Italian Literature" a section devoted to studies of Dante. *Italian Quarterly* has a regular section of book reviews entitled "Dante Shelf" by Thomas G. Bergin, a list of books received, and "Items" (a section devoted to the announcement of reviews and conferences), all of which are bibliographical sources. *Forum Italicum: A*

Quarterly of Italian Studies, a bilingual English-Italian journal published at the State University of New York at Buffalo, includes a regular section of book reviews. *Italica,* the official journal of the American Association of Teachers of Italian, contains a regular "Bibliography of Italian Studies in North America," including sections of bibliography headed "Language, Textbooks, and Pedagogy" and "Dante."

Journals published in Italy with regular sections of bibliography on Dante studies include *L'Alighieri,* a semiannual journal published by the Casa di Dante in Roma with a regular section of annotated bibliography entitled "Rassegna bibliografica dantesca"; *La rassegna della letteratura italiana,* which covers Dante in each of its three issues per year; *Studi danteschi,* an annual journal with annotated notices of new works and an occasional extended section on "Bibliografia dantesca"; and *Il giornale dantesco.* In Germany the annual *Deutsches Dante Jahrbuch* includes articles on Dante primarily, though not exclusively, in German, and an extensive bibliography of works on Dante in many languages.

Useful book-length reviews of criticism in Italian are *Gli studi danteschi dal 1940 al 1949* by Aldo Vallone and *Gli studi danteschi dal 1950 al 1964* by Enzo Esposito.

Finally, the major American library collections of Dante studies are at Cornell and Harvard. Catalogs developed by these libraries, generally available in reference divisions of major libraries, represent another good source of bibliography on Dante.

READING FOR STUDENTS AND TEACHERS

The following survey of background studies and critical works can provide information and suggest directions for classroom presentation of the *Divine Comedy* and serve as the basis of a reading list for students. This discussion confines itself to works available in English, with the exception of basic introductory works. The numerous significant works in Italian and other languages should be consulted whenever possible. Dates in parentheses refer to the original date of publication.

General Introductions to Dante

Many instructors find that the assignment of one general introductory work gives students enough information to guide a first reading. A basic manual directed toward beginning students is *A Handbook to*

Dante Studies (1950) by Umberto Cosmo (*Guida a Dante*, 1950). This work concentrates on helping students to identify the questions relevant to a study of Dante and provides general aids such as a review of important bibliography.

Several comprehensive yet concise one-volume introductions by prominent Dante scholars have appeared in the United States in the past two decades. Francis Fergusson's *Dante* (1966) provides detailed explanations of the facts and ideas surrounding Dante's life and work. Part I is entitled "The Road to the *Commedia*"; Part II, "The *Commedia*." Thomas G. Bergin defines his work *Dante* (1965) as both an introduction for students and a reference for Dantists. Bergin states that his aim is "to present the essential facts of the life and times of Dante Alighieri, to summarize the content of his works, and to suggest . . . his significance for our own century." Allan H. Gilbert's *Dante and His* Comedy (1963), a briefer study than those of Fergusson and Bergin, presents the basic issues necessary for an understanding of the *Divine Comedy* along with an "outline-analysis" of the work. A new volume in the Twayne World Authors Series, *Dante Alighieri* (1979) by Ricardo J. Quinones, provides a comprehensive introduction that takes into account current scholarship. Quinones treats the *Divine Comedy* "in the context of his [Dante's] changeful public career and as the product of his evolving thought and poetic practice."

Another work that can serve as a fine introduction to Dante is Charles H. Grandgent's *Companion to the* Divine Comedy (1975), which Charles S. Singleton excerpted from Grandgent's famous edition of the *Divine Comedy* (1909). The introduction contains twenty concise paragraphs treating significant points of background and biographical information. The arguments for each canto and accompanying notes, along with an index of persons and places mentioned in the poem, occupy the rest of the volume. Also, many teachers find that two volumes by Dorothy Sayers, *Introductory Papers on Dante* (1955) and *Further Papers on Dante* (1957), function well as introductions for undergraduates. In these readable and often witty lectures designed for the general public, Sayers treats the *Divine Comedy* as a "story of adventure" with contemporary significance. The first volume deals with theological and ethical issues, while the second concentrates on literary and poetic matters.

Some teachers find that interpretations addressing the moral and spiritual value of the *Divine Comedy* introduce the poem effectively by providing inspiration for reading. Studies used in this way often involve a personal as well as a scholarly approach. Sister Ruth Mary Fox's *Dante Lights the Way* (1958) treats Dante's work with a religious emphasis, particularly in the final chapter, "The Road to Peace." In *From Hell to Paradise: Dante and His* Comedy (1966), Olaf Lagercrantz presents a reading of the poem as "a life to be lived." Helen M. Luke bases her interpretations in *Dark Wood to White Rose: A Study of Meanings in Dante's* Divine Comedy (1975) on Jungian analyses. Ernest Hatch Wilkins interprets Dante as an "apostle of joy" in *Dante: Poet and Apostle* (1921), while Charles Allen Dinsmore's *The Teachings of Dante* (1901) is known for development of the moral aspects of Dante.

Introductions to Dante in Italian are numerous, but instructors most often cite the following works as accessible and helpful to undergraduates who have mastered Italian: *Dante* (1971) by Nicolò Mineo, *Storia della poesia di Dante* (1962) by Rocco Montano, *Introduzione a Dante* (1975) by Giorgio Padoan, and *La vita, i tempi, e le opere di Dante* (1931) by Nicola Zingarelli. Padoan's work is particularly recommended.

Background Studies

The most problematic task for a teacher of the *Divine Comedy* seems to be the creation of a historical, cultural, literary, and biographical framework to help students organize the sometimes overwhelming multitude of details in the poem. An essential work providing such perspectives is Karl Vossler's *Mediaeval Culture: An Introduction to Dante and His Times* (*Die Göttliche Komödie*, 1907–10), which is considered one of the most important works on Dante of this century. The first volume presents the religious, philosophical, and ethopolitical background, and the second treats the literary background and poetry of the *Divine Comedy*.

Numerous works elaborate the medieval and Renaissance ideas that find expression in Dante. Joseph A. Mazzeo's *Medieval Cultural Tradition in Dante's* Comedy (1960) presents medieval concepts of hierarchy, light metaphysics, analogy, and typology in their role as models for the poem. Marcia L. Colish elaborates the medieval conception of the material world as a sign of spiritual reality in *The Mirror of Language: A Study in the Medieval Theory of Knowledge* (1968). Two useful older studies also treating medieval symbolism are *Medieval Number Symbolism: Its Sources, Meaning, and Influence on Thought and Expression* (1938) by Vincent Forster Hopper and *Symbolism in Medieval Thought and Its Consummation in the* Divine Comedy (1929) by Helen Flanders Dunbar. Joan M. Ferrante devotes a chapter to Dante in *Woman as Image in Medieval Literature: From* the Twelfth Century to Dante (1975), where she demonstrates that Dante incorporates both positive and negative medieval images of women and allows for a feminine aspect of the human soul. In The Symbolic Rose (1960) Barbara Seward discusses the meaning of the rose for Dante in the chapter "The Medieval Heritage." A. Bartlett Giamatti deals with conceptions of paradise and the Golden Age in The Earthly Paradise and the Renaissance Epic (1966), concluding that Dante's gardens, which reflect the condition of the soul, are precursors of the Renaissance conception. A. O. Lovejoy's The Great Chain of Being (1936) contains an explanation of the influential idea of the hierarchy of creation, while Ricardo J. Quinones develops the importance of time for Dante's poem in The Renaissance Discovery of Time (1972). In the chapter "The Western Public and Its Language" in Literary Language and Its Public in Late Latin Antiquity and in the Middle Ages (Literatursprache und Publikum in der lateinische Spätantike und im Mittelalter, 1958) Erich Auerbach traces the development of the concept of an audience with reference to Dante, specifically to his creation of an audience through his direct addresses.

Many general works on the Middle Ages and Renaissance in Europe can help to complete the picture of Dante in his historical context. The Age of Dante: A Concise History of Italian Culture in the Years of the Early Renaissance (1957) by Domenico Vittorini presents a history of the early Italian Renaissance organized around Dante. Ferdinand Schevill's two-volume study, Medieval and Renaissance Florence (1936), is a comprehensive history of the growth of Florence from its founding. Volume I, Medieval Florence, and Volume II, The Coming of Humanism and the Age of the Medici, make extensive reference to Dante. A work celebrating the marvels of Dante's city is Florence in the Age of Dante (1964) by Paul G. Ruggiers, who deals with the life and works of Dante in the chapter "The Three Crowns of Tuscany." Works that place Dante within the medieval literary tradition are W. T. H. Jackson's Medieval Literature: A History and a Guide (1966), which provides introductions to several national traditions in medieval literature, and C. S. Lewis' The Discarded Image: An Introduction to Medieval and Renaissance Literature (1964), which explores the thought and belief of the age. G. G. Coulton's Medieval Panorama: The English Scene from Conquest to Reformation (1938) includes a chapter entitled "Dante's Commedia," which treats the Commedia as a synthesis of medieval thought. Works that place Dante in relation to the visual arts are The Genius of Italy (1954) by Leonardo Olschki, who stresses Dante's impact on Italian art in the essay "Dante and His Circle," and Four Stages of Renaissance Style: Transformations in Art *and Literature, 1400–1700* (1955) by Wylie Sypher, who treats the *Divine Comedy* as a reflection of Gothic art, architecture, and thought.

Dante's largely unfortunate political involvement and his concern for the political future of Italy provided part of the impetus for the *Divine Comedy*. Indeed, some critics, such as Alessandro Passerin d'Entrèves, consider the *Divine Comedy* a political poem. In *Dante as a Political Thinker* (1952), Passerin d'Entrèves explores Dante's attitudes toward the city-state, the empire, and the Church. In *Medieval Political Ideas* (1954) Ewart Lewis presents a section of *De Monarchia* along with an analysis of Dante's political thinking. The essays of Dino Bigongiari included in *Essays on Dante and Medieval Culture* (1964) emphasize political aspects of Dante. *The Crisis in the Early Italian Renaissance: Civic Humanism and Republican Liberty in an Age of Classicism and Tyranny* (1955) by Hans Baron deals with later attitudes toward Dante's concept of government.

Contemporary and early Renaissance views of Dante and his poem can be found in a number of works. David Thompson's compilation, *The Three Crowns of Florence: Humanistic Assessments of Dante, Petrarca, and Boccaccio* (1972), presents a collection of criticism from the fourteenth- and fifteenth-century humanists who both exalted and censured Dante as a "modern." Bernard Weinberg devotes two chapters in *A History of Literary Criticism in the Italian Renaissance* (1961) to "The Quarrel over Dante" while treating the development of criticism in the sixteenth century. J. E. Spingarn's *A History of Literary Criticism in the Renaissance* (1908) also deals with attitudes toward Dante.

Mastery of the *Divine Comedy* necessarily rests on knowledge of the theological, philosophical, and literary sources and antecedents of the poem. In fact, some scholars and teachers maintain that one should not teach Dante without a thorough knowledge of such works as Saint Thomas Aquinas' *Summa Theologica*. Circumstances often unfortunately compel many teachers to begin their teaching of Dante after having read only some of these works, but thorough acquaintance with them is a necessity, and full understanding, a goal. The secondary works on Dante's sources described here are especially appropriate for a course emphasizing the many traditions that converge in the poem.

Dante's chief literary source is Vergil's *Aeneid*, through which Dante received the form of the Homeric epic as well. Several critical works help to place the *Divine Comedy* in the epic tradition. In *Dante's Epic Journeys* (1974) David Thompson maintains that medieval allegorizations of classical epics contribute to the technique of the *Divine Comedy*. Albert Cook in *The Classical Line: A Study in Epic*

Poetry (1967) places the *Divine Comedy* in the tradition of the "refined" epic, while Harold Victor Routh's *God, Man, and Epic Poetry: A Study in Comparative Literature* (1927) treats Dante as an epic poet and the pilgrim as an epic character. W. B. Stanford in *The Ulysses Theme: A Study in the Adaptability of a Traditional Hero* (1954) deals with Dante's portrait of Odysseus in relation to the Homeric tradition. Thomas K. Swing reaches the conclusion that the Holy Trinity rather than Dante the pilgrim is the epic protagonist of the poem in *The Fragile Leaves of the Sybil: Dante's Master Plan* (1962).

In addition to classical works, Dante knew the tradition of Romance literature in the vernacular, which is important as a source of Dante's concept of love. Henry John Chaytor's *The Troubadours of Dante* (1892) provides an anthology of Provençal poets quoted by Dante, such as Brunetto Latini and Bertran de Born, with a substantial introduction on Dante's relation to the troubadours. In *An Essay on the* Vita nuova (1949) Charles S. Singleton distinguishes Dante from the troubadours for his view of Beatrice as a way of reaching God rather than as the goal of his yearning. Charles Williams also explores romantic love as a route to God in *The Figure of Beatrice* (1943). Two significant studies of the tradition of courtly love poetry are C. S. Lewis' *The Allegory of Love: A Study in Medieval Tradition* (1936) and Maurice Valency's *In Praise of Love: An Introduction to the Love Poetry of the Renaissance* (1958). Denis de Rougemont deals with the Christian sublimation of the passions in connection with Dante in the chapter "Sicily, Italy, Beatrice, and Symbols" in *Love in the Western World* (*L'Amour et l'Occident*, 1939). Marianne Shapiro categorizes Dante's portrayals of female figures in *Women, Earthly and Divine, in the* Comedy *of Dante* (1975).

Study of Dante's classical sources proves fruitful in reaching an understanding of Dante. Gilbert Highet devotes the chapter "Dante and Pagan Antiquity" in *The Classical Tradition: Greek and Roman Influences on Western Literature* (1957) to the presence of Aristotle, Vergil, Ovid, Lucan, Cicero, Boethius, and Statius in Dante's works. Ernst Robert Curtius' *European Literature and the Latin Middle Ages* (*Europäische Literatur und lateinisches Mittelalter*, 1953) deals with classical elements in Dante within the context of a broader study of the ancient foundations of Western culture. Charles Till Davis maintains in *Dante and the Idea of Rome* (1957) that the concept of Rome in the *Divine Comedy* unites the pagan and Christian cities, while Allan Gilbert treats Dante's knowledge of Aristotle through Aquinas in *Dante's Conception of Justice* (1925), which provides some of Aquinas' commentaries with an analysis of the *Divine Comedy* as a "poem of justice." Several works deal with both ancient and medieval ideas in Dante: *Dante and the Early Astronomers* (1913) by Mary A. Orr, *Dante and the Animal Kingdom* (1902) by Richard Thayer Holbrook, and *The Treatment of Nature in Dante's* Divina commedia (1897) by L. Oscar Kuhns.

Dante's position in religious and philosophical traditions is difficult to establish. The Bible, to which Dante alludes more than five hundred times in the *Divine Comedy*, is clearly an important source. In *Events and Their Afterlife: The Dialectics of Christian Typology in the Bible and Dante* (1966) A. C. Charity links the techniques of the poem to that of the Bible, maintaining that the *Divine Comedy* represents a subfulfillment of New Testament events while at once looking toward a fulfillment of itself through the conversion of its readers to Christianity. Saint Thomas Aquinas' construct in the *Summa Theologica* is generally considered to be Dante's theological authority, but Philip Henry Wicksteed points out his divergences from it in *Dante and Aquinas* (1913), and Etienne Gilson asserts in *Dante and Philosophy* (1949) that Dante does not follow any system. Some studies of Dante question his doctrinal orthodoxy, such as Kenelm Foster's *The Two Dantes and Other Studies* (1977), which finds both pagan and Christian elements in the *Divine Comedy*. An initially controversial but now accepted view was expressed by Miguel Asín Palacios in *Islam and the* Divine Comedy (*La escatología musulmana en la* Divina comedia, 1919; Eng. trans. 1926), in which he seeks to demonstrate the influence of Islamic models on Dante. Kaufman Kohler relates Dante's views of hell and paradise to various Near Eastern traditions in *Heaven and Hell in Comparative Religion* (1923), and Edmund Garratt Gardner traces the influence of mystics beginning with Augustine in *Dante and the Mystics* (1913).

Biographies provide yet another avenue to understanding the context of the *Divine Comedy*. Probably because little is known about Dante's life, relatively few major biographies have been written. Giovanni Boccaccio (1313?–1375) wrote the first biography of Dante within fifty years of his death, and Leonardo Bruni Aretino (1369–1444) followed soon afterward with the next significant biography. Even these early accounts leave many points in dispute. The Boccaccio and Aretino biographies are available in a translation by James Robinson Smith entitled *The Earliest Lives of Dante* (1901), which also contains a passage from a biography by Filippo Villani (d. 1405?), "The Embassy to Florence." An important twentieth-century study, Michele Barbi's *Life of Dante* (*Dante: vita, opere, e fortuna,* 1933; Eng. trans. 1954), which portrays Dante as a man of vision who sought to redeem his contemporaries through his own faith, is a brief yet complete biography appropriate for assignment to undergraduates. The final chapter of Barbi's work presents a short historical analysis of Dante's reputation in Italy. The most recent biography in English is *Dante and His World* (1967) by Thomas Caldecot Chubb. This quite extensive and very readable work draws evidence from a wide range of sources, including Dante's own writings, to support the assertion that three forces formed Dante's character: his love for Beatrice, his exile, and his loss of belief in the possibility of an ideal empire.

Critical Works

An introduction to the changing emphases of critical interpretation and to the importance of Dante for other authors not only fosters comprehension of the poem but also encourages students to develop their own critical and artistic responses. This section groups critical works in several categories: works on issues concerning the style and structure of the entire poem, studies of Dante's influences on particular writers and in various literary traditions, works devoted to individual canticles, and critical materials available in collections.

Much critical debate in this century has centered on the relation between poetry and philosophy in the *Divine Comedy*. A trend toward the separation of poetry and philosophy began in Italian criticism with Francesco De Sanctis (1817–83). Following Giambattista Vico's idea that poetry and philosophy are antithetical, De Sanctis stressed the poetic aspects of the *Divine Comedy* and advocated reading it without a commentary. A selection of De Sanctis' criticism is available in *De Sanctis on Dante* (1959), edited by Joseph Rossi and Alfred Galpin. The essay "The Subject of the *Divine Comedy*" introduces effectively the magic and wonder of the poem and provides a definition of Dante's poetic achievement. One of De Sanctis' disciples, Benedetto Croce (1866–1952), went on to advocate the distillation of the poetry from the theological framework he considered dry and irrelevant. This controversial and influential theory can be found in *The Poetry of Dante* (*La poesia di Dante*, 1920).

The mainstream of criticism has sought to demonstrate the interrelatedness of poetry and philosophy in the *Divine Comedy*. In his well-known essays, *Three Philosophical Poets: Lucretius, Dante, and Goethe* (1910), George Santayana maintained that philosophy and poetry are coterminous in Dante's work, and Ezra Pound emphasized the relevance of allegory to poetry in his treatment of Dante in *The Spirit of Romance* (1910). Pound called Dante to the attention of T. S.

Eliot, who steered a median critical course by advocating an initial consideration of the poetry alone and the completion of the philosophical and theological framework afterward in *Dante* (1929). Irma Brandeis' *The Ladder of Vision: A Study of Dante's* Comedy (1960), a work often assigned in introductory courses, opposes the Crocean view, maintaining that Dante's poetry fuses abstract theory with experience in this life.

Twentieth-century criticism has also addressed the related issue of the nature of Dante's allegory. Most critics have concluded that Dante wrote some version of the "allegory of theologians," the fourfold form of allegory in which the literal level is considered true, rather than the "allegory of poets," a twofold allegory that builds on a fictional base. This critical trend received impetus from Erich Auerbach's important study *Dante, Poet of the Secular World* (*Dante als Dichter der irdischen Welt*, 1929), which stresses Dante's representation of man's concrete historical reality on this earth. Two prominent American Dante scholars, Charles S. Singleton and Robert Hollander, have developed the implications of Auerbach's view for Dante's allegorical method. In *Dante Studies 1* (1954) and *Dante Studies 2* (1958) Singleton defines Dante's poem as an analogue of the "poem" of the world created by God. Hollander explores the "allegorical theory and practice" of the poem in *Allegory in Dante's* Commedia (1969), concluding that Dante's principle of composition derives from medieval methods of interpreting the scriptures. Giuseppe Mazzotta treats the subject of allegory in relation to Dante's attitude toward history in *Dante, Poet of the Desert: History and Allegory in the* Divine Comedy (1979), demonstrating that Dante's allegory is composed of intertwined and interdependent strands of secular and sacred history. John G. Demaray in *The Invention of Dante's* Commedia (1974) maintains that the literal level of Dante's journey is patterned on medieval pilgrimages to the Holy Land, while Sheila Ralphs explores the progression of selected images and symbols in *Dante's Journey to the Center: Some Patterns in His Allegory* (1973).

While Croce's complete exclusion of philosophy has been challenged by most critics, his work called attention to the aesthetic qualities of Dante's poem, thereby opening the way for consideration of Dante's stylistic accomplishments. Glauco Cambon's essays in *Dante's Craft: Studies in Language and Style* (1969) deal with Dante's concept and use of language, which, Cambon asserts, Dante regarded as mankind's most significant achievement. In *From Image to Idea: A Study of the Simile in Dante's* Commedia (1977), Richard H. Lansing defines several functions for Dante's similes, expanding beyond T. S. Eliot's idea that they serve only for explanation. Patrick Boyde treats Dante's individual style in a theoretical way that illuminates the *Divine Comedy* as well as the *Rime* in *Dante's Style in His Lyric Poetry* (1971).

Reception and Influence Studies

A work as powerful as the *Divine Comedy* inevitably enters into the creation of other literature, and much of Western literature has been touched in some way by Dante. Some of the most important poets of the twentieth century, such as W. B. Yeats, T. S. Eliot, and Ezra Pound, have learned poetic techniques from Dante, and numerous novelists, including James Joyce, Thomas Mann, and Albert Camus, have recreated or developed characters, themes, or structure from the *Divine Comedy*. Dante has provided images for some American black writers, such as Ralph Ellison in *Invisible Man* and Leroi Jones, who uses the categories of the *Inferno* in his novel *The System of Dante's Hell*. Study of works indebted to Dante can be a stimulus to study of the *Divine Comedy*, and many instructors include such works on the reading list or devote class discussion to them. Critical works on Dante's influence and reception can help in the location of works appropriate to a particular course.

Most critics dealing with Dante's use by other writers explore parallels and similarities as well as influence. A number of works make a connection between Dante and Milton. Irene Samuel bases her discussion of "echoes, analogues, and parallels" in *Dante and Milton: The Commedia and Paradise Lost* (1966) on Milton's reading of and comments on Dante. In *Dante, Michelangelo, and Milton* (1963) John Arthos relates three artists through what he considers their fulfillment of Longinus' notion of the sublime, in Dante's case his depiction of the union between man and God. S. Humphries Gurteen compares three depictions of hell in *The Epic of the Fall of Man: A Comparative Study of Caedmon, Dante, and Milton* (1896). Dante's influence on Chaucer is also significant. Howard Schless discusses the nature and degree of influence and compares specific passages in *Dante and Chaucer* (1981). In *Trope and Allegory: Themes Common to Dante and Shakespeare* (1977), Francis Fergusson maintains that Dante and Shakespeare found their creations in the same storehouse of Christian and classical themes. Marion Montgomery sees in Dante the beginnings of the Romantic movement in *The Reflective Journey toward Order* (1973), while Pietro Cali deals with the visionary element in *Allegory and Vision in Dante and Langland* (1971). Book-length studies dealing with Dante's presence in modern poetry are *Dante and Pound: The Epic of Judgement* (1974) by James J. Wilhelm, who identifies a profound influence of Dante on *The Cantos;* and *Montale and Dante* (1968) by Arshi Pipa, who finds that Dante serves this modern Italian poet as a model. Mary T. Reynolds thoroughly documents Dante's importance for James Joyce in a comprehensive work, *Dante and Joyce* (1981).

Numerous works deal with Dante's reception in various nations and his influence in national literary traditions. American students might be particularly interested in a chronicle of Dante's fortunes in the United States by Angelina LaPiana, *Dante's American Pilgrimage: A Historical Survey of Dante Studies in the United States, 1800–1944* (1948). Paget Toynbee studies the relation between Dante and English literature in *Dante in English Literature from Chaucer to Cary* (1909), and A. L. Sells's *The Italian Influence in English Poetry from Chaucer to Southwell* (1955) contains ample mention of Dante in this period. Mario Praz also develops Anglo-Italian literary relations in *The Flaming Heart: Essays on Crashaw, Machiavelli, and Other Studies in the Relations between Italian and English Literature from Chaucer to T. S. Eliot* (1958), which includes the chapter "T. S. Eliot and Dante" as well as reference to Dante in "Chaucer and Great Italian Writers of Trecento." A work with a wider range is Werner P. Friederich's *Dante's Fame Abroad, 1350–1850: The Influence of Dante Alighieri on the Poets and Scholars of Spain, France, England, Germany, Switzerland, and the U.S.* (1950). In connection with the seventh centennial of Dante's birth Vittore Branca and Ettore Caccia edited a volume entitled *Dante nel mondo* (1965), which includes essays in Italian by various authors on Dante's influence throughout the world.

Studies of Individual Canticles

Most of the book-length works on the *Inferno* date from the early twentieth century, but some of these early studies remain helpful. M. Alice Wyld's *The Dread* Inferno: *Notes for Beginners in the Study of Dante* (1904), a general introduction and explication, and William H. V. Reade's analysis of the sins and punishments, *The Moral System of Dante's* Inferno (1909), have recently been reprinted. The essays in Mark Musa's *Advent at the Gates: Dante's* Comedy (1974), which grew from his experiences in the classroom, concentrate on the *Inferno:* "A Lesson in Lust," "Behold Francesca Who Speaks So Well," "From Measurement to Meaning: Simony," "At the Gates of Dis," "In the Valley of the Princes," and "The 'Sweet New Style' That I Hear."

Wallace Fowlie bases *A Reading of Dante's* Inferno (1981) on a lifetime of teaching and studying the *Divine Comedy*.

The *Purgatorio*, which for its portrayal of progress has been called the most modern of the canticles, is the focus of two important recent studies. In *Dante's Drama of the Mind: A Modern Reading of the* Purgatorio (1953) Francis Fergusson describes the "developing form of the poem" through a discussion of the *Purgatorio*, the canticle where he believes Dante presents most completely the drama of creation for Dante the poet and of discovery for Dante the pilgrim. Another excellent study is Bernard Stambler's *Dante's Other World: The* Purgatorio *as Guide to the* Divine Comedy (1957). The first chapter, "Environs of the *Commedia*," introduces the issues and opinions concerning Dante, while the remaining chapters, organized around the *Purgatorio* as the center of the *Divine Comedy*, take up matters related to the complete poem.

A number of studies can help with explication of what many regard as the most difficult canticle, the *Paradiso*. In *Structure and Thought in the* Paradiso (1958) Joseph A. Mazzeo explores concepts such as love, beauty, and beatitude in the *Paradiso* in relation to the classical tradition as well as the structural principles of the canticle. Robin Kirkpatrick stresses the magnitude and originality of Dante's poetic task in *Dante's* Paradiso *and the Limitations of Modern Criticism: A Study of Style and Poetic Theory* (1975). Sheila Ralphs treats imagery in *Etterno Spiro: A Study in the Nature of Dante's* Paradiso (1962), while Howard Needler concentrates on two figures in *Saint Francis and Saint Dominic in the* Divine Comedy (1969). A valuable older study is Edmund G. Gardner's *Dante's Ten Heavens: A Study of the* Paradiso (1898), an introduction based in part on medieval commentaries.

Collections of Essays

For a useful overview of Dante criticism, one should consult the many anthologies of essays and articles on the *Divine Comedy*. Such collections are particularly helpful for providing the nonspecialist with access to prominent Italian critics such as Bruno Nardi, Natalino Sapegno, and Giorgio Petrocchi, whose longer works have not been translated into English.

John Freccero's *Dante: A Collection of Critical Essays* (1965) includes many important articles. In his introduction Freccero explains the critical and historical significance of the essays he incorporates in his collection: "The Survival and Transformation of Dante's Vision of

Reality" by Erich Auerbach; "The Poetry of Dante" by Luigi Pirandello; "The *Vita nuova*" by T. S. Eliot; "Introduction to Dante's *Rime*" by Gianfranco Contini; "Dante and Medieval Culture" by Bruno Nardi; "The Mind in Love: Dante's Philosophy" by Kenelm Foster, O.P.; "Paolo and Francesca" by Renato Poggioli; "Speech and Language in *Inferno* XIII" by Leo Spitzer; " 'In Exitu Israel de Aegypto' " by Charles S. Singleton; "Dante's *DXV*" by R. E. Kaske; "*Civitas*" by Alessando Passerin d'Entrèves; "The Metamorphoses of the Circle" by Georges Poulet; "The Recollection of the Way" by Charles Williams.

Robert J. Clements has edited a volume, *American Critical Essays on* The Divine Comedy (1967), celebrating the American contribution to Dante scholarship, which includes "The Living Dante" by Ernest Hatch Wilkins; "Dante's Hundred Cantos" by Allan H. Gilbert; "Dante's Terza Rima" by J. S. P. Tatlock; "Dante's Addresses to the Reader" by Erich Auerbach; "Reminiscence and Anticipation in the *Divine Comedy*" by Ernest Hatch Wilkins; "The Art of Dante's *Purgatorio*" by Helmut Hatzfeld; "Dante's Allegory" by Charles S. Singleton; "Typological Symbolism in Medieval Literature" by Erich Auerbach; "On the Personae of the *Comedy*" by Thomas G. Bergin; "Rex Iustus et Pius: Henry's Throne and Dante's Christian Prince" by Theodore Silverstein; "Dante's Conception of Love" by Joseph Anthony Mazzeo; "The Wrath of Dante" by Guiseppe Antonio Borgese; "Voices of the *Divine Comedy*" by Ernest Hatch Wilkins; "Dante's Prophetic Morning-Dreams" by Charles Speroni; "Modern Literary Scholarship as Reflected in Dante Criticism" by Helmut Hatzfeld; "Dante after Seven Centuries" by Robert J. Clements.

Mark Musa's collection *Essays on Dante* (1964) contains a translation of "Dante's Letter to Can Grande" by Nancy Howe; "Allegory" by Charles S. Singleton; "Hell: Topography and Demography" by Thomas G. Bergin; "The Wrath of Dante" by G. A. Borgese; "Farinata and Cavalcante" by Erich Auerbach; "Aesthetic Structure in the *Inferno*, Canto XIX" by Mark Musa; "The Farcical Elements in *Inferno*, Cantos XXI–XXIII" by Leo Spitzer; "The Character of Dante and His Utopia" by Francesco De Sanctis.

Irma Brandeis has edited a collection, *Discussions of the* Divine Comedy (1961), that gives a picture of the historical development of criticism of the *Divine Comedy*. Part I, "Before the Twentieth Century," presents excerpts from discussions of Dante by Giovanni Boccaccio, Petrarch, Giambattista Vico, Voltaire, Samuel Taylor Coleridge, Ugo Foscolo, Goethe, John Ruskin, and Giosuè Carducci. The essays in Part II, "The Twentieth Century," include "Genesis and

Composition of the *Divine Comedy"* by Michele Barbi; "Aesthetic Criteria" by Benedetto Croce; "The Substantive Penchant" by Luigi Malagoli; "Figural Art in the *Divine Comedy"* by Erich Auerbach; "Hell" by Philip H. Wicksteed; "The Metaphor of the Journey" by Francis Fergusson; "The Pattern at the Center" by Charles S. Singleton; "The Transfiguration of Beatrice" by Etienne Gilson; "The 'Three Blessed Ladies' of the *Divine Comedy"* by Jefferson B. Fletcher; "The Symbolic Imagination: A Meditation on Dante's Three Mirrors" by Allen Tate; and " A Talk on Dante" by T. S. Eliot.

The lectures collected by Thomas G. Bergin in *From Time to Eternity: Essays on Dante's* Divine Comedy (1967) were delivered at Yale University in 1965: "How the *Commedia* Was Born" by Natalino Sapegno; "Dante and the Florence of the Good Old Days" by Rafaello Morghen; "Dante and Thirteenth-Century Asceticism" by Giorgio Petrocchi; "Dante's Idea of Love" by Kenelm Foster, O.P.; "Dramas of Selfhood in the *Comedy"* by Thomas H. Greene; and "Imagery and Thematic Patterns in *Paradiso* XXIII" by Aldo Scaglione.

The Mind of Dante (1965), edited by Uberto Limentani, includes lectures delivered at the University of Cambridge in 1965: "Genesis and Structure: Two Approaches to the Poetry of the *Comedy"* by Natalino Sapegno; "The Poetry of the *Comedy"* by P. McNair; "Religion and Philosophy in Dante" by Kenelm Foster, O.P.; "Dante's Lyric Poetry" by Patrick Boyde; "Dante's Political Thought" by Uberto Limentani; "Dante's Views on Language" by J. Cremona; "Dante and the English Poets" by C. P. Brand.

The studies in *A Dante Symposium* (1965), edited by William J. DeSua and Gino Rizzo, include "Dante's Style and Gothic Aesthetic" by Rocco Montano; "Ueber die *Vita nuova"* by Ulrich Leo; "Dante's *Divine Comedy:* The View from God's Eye" by Aldo Bernardo; "Features of the Poetic Language of the *Divina commedia"* by Helmut Hatzfeld; "Metrical Patterns in the *Divine Comedy"* by George H. Gifford; "Dante's Noble Sinners: Abstract Examples or Living Characters?" by Glauco Cambon; "Beatrice in Dante's Plot" by Allan H. Gilbert; "Dante and the Virtuous Pagans" by Gino Rizzo; "The *Altra Via* and Guido as *Attendant Lord"* by John Mahoney; " 'There is a Place Down there . . .' (*Inferno* XXIV)" by Mark Musa; "*Il peregrin e i navicanti* di *Purgatorio* VIII. 1–6" by Giovanni Cecchetti; "Dante and Islam: History and Analysis of a Controversy" by Vicente Cantarino; "Dante and Italian Nationalism" by Charles T. Davis.

S. Bernard Chandler and J. A. Molinaro edited *The World of Dante: Six Studies in Language and Thought* (1966), which presents "Dante and the Drama of Language" by Glauco Cambon; "The River of

Death: *Inferno* II. 108" by John Freccero; "The Living Poet and the
Myth of Time: Christian Comedy" by John F. Mahoney; "Dante's
Three Communities: Mediation and Order" by Joseph Anthony Maz-
zeo; "Dante's Katabasis and Mission" by Gian Roberto Sarolli; "The
Twins of Latona" by Erich von Richthofen.

The articles in *A Dante Profile* (1967), edited by Franca Schettino,
include "The *Vita nuova* and Commentary" by Norma L. Goodrich;
"Folklore in the *Divine Comedy*" by Charles Speroni; "The Dante of
T. S. Eliot" by John J. Bullaro; "Dante Profile in Italian Literature" by
Franca Schettino.

AIDS TO TEACHING

The teaching of the *Divine Comedy* can be enhanced with a wealth
of art works, for the poem has inspired artists and composers throughout the centuries. In the area of visual arts, portraits of the poet, illuminated manuscripts, illustrated editions, and individual paintings,
drawings, and sculpture can help students to form conceptions of
characters and episodes in the poem.

Dante's image is already familiar to many students, for he has been
represented often in painting and sculpture. No faithful likeness of
him is known to exist, however. Two paintings by contemporaries, who
theoretically could have created faithful portraits from firsthand knowledge, have been destroyed or damaged: fire consumed a portrait by
Taddeo Gaddi in Santa Croce, Florence, in 1566, and restorers disfig-
ured a portrait by Giotto (or a follower) in the Bargello in Florence. In
Portraits of Dante from Giotto to Raffael: A Critical Study (1911)
Richard Thayer Holbrook concludes that only Giotto's portrait records
Dante's features rather than his fame. Although current thinking con-
tradicts some of his attributions, Holbrook's work is of interest for its
approach and numerous plates.

The discovery in Ravenna in 1865 of Dante's skeleton led to comparisons of the skull with portraits and sculptures. One such study is
The Portraits of Dante (1921) by Frank Jewett Mather, who concludes
that the most faithful portrait is the so-called Palatine Miniature,
which he considers a copy of a lost portrait by Taddeo Gaddi. This
book contains discussion of the various traditions in the iconography of
Dante with illustrations. The spring 1965 issue of *Italian Quarterly*
contains a color inset entitled "A Selection from Dante's Iconography" and features numerous color reproductions of portraits.

Illustrators began to prepare illuminated manuscripts of the *Divine Comedy* during Dante's lifetime, producing hundreds before the first printed version of the *Comedy* in 1481. Commentators speculate that Dante valued the art of illumination, for in the *Purgatorio* the pilgrim encounters Oderisi, an illuminator who sadly admits that the pages of another artist "smile" more than his own (*Purg.* XI. 79–87). His placement of Oderisi among the proud, however, reveals the attitude toward illumination of Dante's contemporaries, who considered illustration an intrusion into the text.

The definitive study of the illustrated manuscripts is *Illuminated Manuscripts of the* Divine Comedy (1969) by Peter Brieger, Millard Meiss, and Charles S. Singleton. Volume I contains introductory essays by the authors, an analysis of the illustrations by canto, a catalog of important illustrated manuscripts of the *Divine Comedy*, a section of comparative illustrations, a bibliography, and indexes. Volume II includes more than eleven hundred illustrations from the fourteenth to the sixteenth century reproduced in black-and-white and color.

Numerous postmedieval artists have also accepted the challenge of creating illustrations for the *Divine Comedy*. The best-known series of drawings available in recent editions are those of Sandro Botticelli, John Flaxman, William Blake, and Gustave Doré.

Botticelli's drawings, begun in 1481 for a member of the Medici family, reveal close attention to the poem, although some find that they lack its intensity. The British art historian Kenneth Clark prepared a substantial introduction for a volume of the ninety-two drawings entitled *The Drawings by Sandro Botticelli for Dante's* Divine Comedy (1976).

John Flaxman's illustrated Dante, *La* Divina commedia *di Dante*, was first published in Rome in 1793. The outline drawings (thirty-eight for the *Inferno*, thirty-nine for the *Purgatorio*, thirty-three for the *Paradiso*) are neoclassical in style. A recent edition of these drawings, *Flaxman's Designs for Dante:* Inferno, Purgatorio, Paradiso (1968), edited by Bill Tate, includes portions of the poem in translation by Ichabod Charles Wright.

William Blake learned Italian at the age of sixty-seven to read the *Divine Comedy* for his drawings, commissioned in 1824. Although Blake does not mention Dante in his poetry, some critics have seen affinities between the poets. W. B. Yeats, for example, makes comparisons in "William Blake and His Illustrations to the *Divine Comedy*," an 1897 essay printed in *Essays and Introductions* as well as other collections. Blake's drawings can be obtained in *Illustrations to the* Divine Comedy (1968), a reprint of a 1922 limited edition, and in

Albert S. Roe's *Blake's Illustrations to the* Divine Comedy (1953). Roe's introduction to the drawings provides substantial commentary on the background and nature of the drawings.

Gustave Doré's drawings, seventy-six for the *Inferno* and sixty for the *Purgatorio* and *Paradiso* together, first appeared in 1861. Doré's Dante, an elderly and severe figure, wears the traditional laurel wreath. Doré's contemporaries thought his depictions of the tortures of hell particularly effective. Although now out of print, the Lawrence Grant White translation of the *Divine Comedy* (1948), with a selection of Doré's drawings, is widely available in libraries.

A number of contemporary American artists have created illustrations for one or more cantos of the *Divine Comedy*, and these are currently available in deluxe editions. In *Drawings for Dante's* Inferno (1963) by Federico Lebrun, portions of the *Inferno* in translation by John Ciardi face thirty-six plates. Ciardi praises these drawings in his introduction for their expression of Dante's meaning through the human form alone. Robert Rauschenberg brought the techniques of post–abstract expressionism to his illustrations of the *Inferno* in *Thirty-four Drawings for Dante's* Inferno (1964). The graphic artist Leonard Baskin illustrated an oversize edition of the translation by Thomas G. Bergin, *The Divine Comedy* (1969), with 120 black-and-white wash line drawings characterized by distended human forms.

While illustrators generally have tackled the entire *Divine Comedy*, artists selecting individual episodes for representation have often elected to concentrate on the *Inferno*. Some believe that the *Inferno* is the only canticle appropriate for visual interpretation because of its sensual, pictorial imagery and that the *Purgatorio* and *Paradiso*, where space often attains meaning through reference to abstractions, escape the artist's reach.

Works of art on subjects from the *Divine Comedy* number in the thousands, but reproductions of the minor works are difficult to locate. The following listing by canticle and canto treats only works of artistic significance in themselves that are frequently reproduced in books on the artist's work or in publications of the institution owning the work.

Inferno II: Jean-Baptiste Camille Corot's *Dante and Vergil* (1859), an oil painting in the Boston Art Museum, depicts Dante and Vergil confronting the three beasts.

Inferno V: Many first-rate artists have devoted attention to the Paolo and Francesca episode. Jean Auguste Dominique Ingres made several oil paintings of the scene. The Louvre in Paris displays his *Francesca da Rimini* (1818), while the Hyde Collection in Glens Falls, New York, owns another version of it. Also in the Louvre is *The Shades of Francesca da Rimini and Her Lover Appearing to Dante and Vergil* (1821), an oil painting by Ary Scheffer. Auguste Rodin originally designed his *Baiser* (*The Kiss*, 1886) as a representation of Paolo and Francesca for his *Gates of Hell* (1880–1917), an unfinished bronze door in the Rodin Museum in Paris projected to feature 128 figures from the *Inferno*.

Inferno VIII: Eugène Delacroix's oil painting in the Louvre, *Dante and Vergil Crossing the Lake That Encircles the City of Dis Guarded by Phlegyas* (1822), also called *The Bark of Dante*, depicts Dante and Vergil surrounded by a threatening sea.

Inferno XXXIII: Jean Baptiste Carpeaux's *Ugolino and His Sons* (1865–76), a sculpture of a seated Ugolino surrounded by his four emaciated sons, can be seen in the Metropolitan Museum of Art in New York. Rodin also sculpted the subject in *Ugolino* (1882).

Inferno, Purgatorio, Paradiso: The city that sent Dante into exile commissioned Domenico di Michelino to paint a tribute, *Dante and His Poem* (1465), to commemorate the second centenary of his birth. In this oil painting in the Duomo in Florence, Dante stands in the foreground presenting the three realms of the afterlife to his native city. Many commentators consider Michelangelo's fresco in the Sistine Chapel at the Vatican in Rome, *The Last Judgment* (1541), Dantesque in spirit, particularly the figures of Minos and Charon. Michelangelo illustrated the *Purgatorio* in a series of marginal drawings that have been lost.

A great deal of music also takes inspiration from the *Divine Comedy*. The following presents only a few of the best-known of these musical compositions, many of which have been frequently recorded. (Consult the monthly *Schwann Record and Tape Guide* for a listing of current recordings.)

Inferno III: Dante was neglected, while Petrarch was favored, by composers until the end of the sixteenth century, when several madrigalists found inspiration in Dante's onomatopoetic re-creation of the cacophony beyond the Gate of Hell (*Inf.* III. 22–27). Luzzascho Luzzaschi, organist for Duke Alfonso II of Ferrara, composed one of his most innovative madrigals in five parts, "Quivi sospiri," on Dante's lines. An excerpt of the madrigal appears in *The Madrigal* by Jerome Roche, and the entire setting can be found in Volume VII of *The Golden Age of the Madrigal*.

Inferno V: The Paolo and Francesca episode has been treated musically more than any other passage in the *Divine Comedy*, with more than twenty-five operas devoted to the subject. Among the most significant compositions are *Fantasy on Francesca da Rimini* (1876), an orchestral work by Peter Ilich Tchaikovsky; *Francesca da Rimini* (1906), an opera by Sergei Rachmaninoff; and *Francesca da Rimini* (1914), an opera by Riccardo Zandonai based on Gabriele D'Annunzio's play of the same title.

Inferno XXX: Giacomo Puccini's *Trittico* (1908), a trilogy of one-act operas, includes *Gianni Schicchi,* a comedy involving the legend Dante relates in the *bolgia* of the falsifiers (*Inf.* XXX. 31–45).

Paradiso XXXIII: Saint Bernard's prayers to the Virgin in *Par.* XXXIII. 1–21 is the only setting of the *Divine Comedy* known to have been composed during Dante's lifetime. That rendering exists only in manuscript form. Giuseppe Verdi scored these lines for a four-part a cappella women's chorus or quartet in "Laudi alla Vergine Maria," one of his *Four Sacred Pieces* (1898).

Divine Comedy: Franz Liszt composed his *Dante Sonata* in the late 1830s, labeling it a "Dantesque fragment." His *Dante Symphony* (1856), considered one of his major orchestral works, re-creates the atmosphere of the three canticles in movements entitled "Inferno," "Purgatorio," and "Magnificat."

Recordings of readings of the *Divine Comedy* can be useful for enabling students to experience Dante's poetry through sound. Available recordings feature John Ciardi reading the first eight cantos of his translation of the *Inferno* (Folkways FL 9871) and Professor Enrico De' Negri reading the first eight cantos of the *Inferno* in Italian (Folkways FL 9977). A series of cassettes devoted to masterpieces of world literature includes lectures on Dante by prominent teachers and scholars: "Dante and Machiavelli" by Anne Paolucci and "The Divine Comedy" by John Freccero.

FURTHER READING ON TEACHING DANTE

Teachers concerned with teaching the Italian language might wish to look at an article by William F. Bottiglia, "Dante at M.I.T.: A New Pedagogical Approach." Bottiglia describes in detail a course developed to teach students with no previous knowledge of Italian to read the entire *Divine Comedy* in Italian in two semesters. The method involves nine weeks of intensive work in Italian grammar and pronunciation, with the remainder of the time devoted to reading five cantos each week.

A volume edited by Haskell Block, *The Teaching of World Literature: Proceedings of the Conference on the Teaching of World Litera-*

ture, University of Wisconsin, 1959, assembles fourteen papers on teaching literature in translation in introductory world literature courses. Several of the essays mention teaching the *Divine Comedy.*

Finally, the teacher of the *Divine Comedy* should be familiar with the articles on pedagogy regularly published in *Italica,* the journal of the American Association of Teachers of Italian, as well as with the publications and activities of the American Dante Society, which grew from meetings of the Dante Club in Cambridge, Massachusetts, initiated by Henry Wadsworth Longfellow. Of particular interest to instructors of Dante is the society's annual Dante Prize, awarded each year since 1887 to the best essay submitted by an undergraduate on the life or works of the poet. The society also offers a similar award for the best essay by a graduate student, the Charles Hall Grandgent Award (for further information, consult the society's journal, *Dante Studies*).

Part Two

APPROACHES

INTRODUCTION

The authors of the essays that follow were invited to write about one or more aspects of their teaching of Dante's *Divine Comedy*—the organization and development of their courses or units, as well as the approaches, techniques, methods, and activities they use to achieve the goals of their courses. Many of the writers remarked that the task of writing about their teaching was a new one, both delightful and difficult, and a salutary one, they felt, because it helped them to clarify the principles of their own pedagogy.

Part II begins with an introductory essay by Giovanni Cecchetti. In the essay, which he described as "teaching in action," Cecchetti identifies nine key points that can structure and inform an initial reading of the *Divine Comedy*. The other essays are grouped according to their emphases in the following categories: Philosophies of Teaching and Reading the *Divine Comedy*, Critical Approaches to Teaching the *Divine Comedy*, and Selected Courses and Units on Dante: Pedagogical Strategies.

The pilgrim's process of learning and his guides' methods of teaching are important subjects of the *Divine Comedy*; furthermore, Dante, perhaps to a greater extent than most other writers, takes on the role of teacher to all of his readers. The *Divine Comedy* in a sense, then, contains instruction on teaching, and the authors of the essays in Philosophies of Teaching and Reading the *Divine Comedy* derive their views of teaching and learning the *Divine Comedy* from the insights within the text, as well as from the nature of the text itself. Glauco Cambon explores the dynamic relation between student and teacher dramatized by Dante and Vergil. He urges teachers of the *Divine Comedy* to emulate Vergil's didactic style and thus to encourage students to learn from experience as well as through intellectual discourse. Richard Lansing gives similar counsel: since the *Divine Comedy* reveals its meanings gradually, through successive images, the poem must be experienced as well as explained. Wallace Fowlie praises the timelessness and completeness of Dante's unique literary achievement and compares Dante's work to that of Joyce and Proust.

Instructors seem to feel free to call on the resources of any useful critical approach to the *Divine Comedy* in the classroom, depending on the passage involved. In fact, the multiplicity of layers of meaning in the *Divine Comedy* seems nearly to preclude the exclusive use of one approach for teaching. At the same time, precisely because of the abundance of material in the work, many instructors find that concentration on one approach or another helps them to establish a foundation of understanding upon which students can build their knowledge of the work in its complexity. The choice of approach, of course, is bound up with the instructor's goal and the nature of the course.

Each of the essays in Critical Approaches to Teaching the *Divine Comedy* describes the use of a particular critical approach, explaining both the principles and the practice of teaching through the approach. Christopher Kleinhenz presents the textual method, relating it closely to linguistic, rhetorical, and stylistic approaches. In the context of a general description of her courses on Dante, Rachel Jacoff details the typological and intertextual approach, which she connects to the theological and historical contexts of the poem. Drawing on Jungian psychology as well as mythology and anthropology, Gaetano Cipolla presents the archetypal approach. Marie Giuriceo describes her treatment of the *Divine Comedy* from a comparative perspective in a survey of masterpieces of Western literature. The essay by Philip Gallagher deals with a textual approach geared to five specific interpretive rules.

In Selected Courses and Units on Dante: Pedagogical Strategies, the essays develop the progress from start to finish of a unit or course devoted to Dante's *Divine Comedy*. The authors present such aspects of their pedagogical approaches as the formulation and communication of goals, methods of lecture and discussion, and types of assignments and examinations. In addition to presenting the teacher's point of view on the work, these writers provide a good deal of insight into students' reactions, both impulsive and informed, to Dante's poem.

These essays describe a wide variety of courses that include the *Divine Comedy*. Three of these teachers present courses in which they concentrate on one of the canticles. Judith Kollmann treats the *Paradiso* as a definition of the essence of Western medieval art in a course devoted to Eastern and Western medieval literature; Elizabeth R. Hatcher teaches the *Purgatorio* as one unit of a course on medieval literature; Theodora Graham approaches the *Inferno* through its relation to art and architecture in the second semester of a course in the Western tradition. John B. Harcourt devotes a freshman seminar to the three canticles of the *Divine Comedy*, drawing on modern philosophy, theology, and literature for the development of literary understanding and moral values. Sister Mary Clemente Davlin describes her one-semester course on the *Divine Comedy*, in which she overcomes the unfamiliarity of the poem through a concentration on the literal, psychological, and religious interpretations as well as through numerous exercises and experiences outside the classroom. The structure of a one-semester course covering the complete *Divine Comedy* is outlined also by Robert Hollander. Amilcare Iannucci describes an approach to the *Divine Comedy* that seeks to mediate the cultural, historical, and linguistic features that divide the poem from students of today.

One of the threads running through all the essays is the belief that Dante can be accessible and enjoyable to college students at every level whether or not they are literature or language majors. At the same time, the writers recognize that true understanding of the *Divine Comedy* exacts extraordinary preparation, discipline, intelligence, and work from both students and teachers, and the courses described are rigorous with regard to reading assigned and comprehension expected. Finally, all the essays communicate the pleasure of knowing and teaching the *Divine Comedy*, important elements in any course certainly but perhaps essential ones for a course on Dante.

CS

AN INTRODUCTION TO DANTE'S *DIVINE COMEDY*

Giovanni Cecchetti

What is a classic? The answer to that question is at once very simple and very complex: A classic is a text that has a permanent significance, or carries a permanent message, for all generations; its words remain always the same, but their meanings slowly change by adapting themselves to the needs and aspirations of the various ages, as we ride on the rhythm of time. In other words, a classic is a text that never belongs to the past but always to the present, and that is, therefore, always contemporary, a text in which human beings, precisely because they are human beings, keep rediscovering themselves.

In this sense, no work of the past is more of a classic than Dante's *Divine Comedy*. Its richness of images, its many levels of meaning, its wealth of themes, its great abundance of people speaking to us from the various rungs of the ladder of pain and joy, make it a world unto itself, but its men and women are essentially like us, in their compulsions as well as in their aspirations. In this essay I hope to point out a small portion of that richness by touching on some of the poem's meanings and their ramifications and by recalling, however briefly, some of its themes and characters with the purpose of offering a swift, but not cursory, overview of the substance of this classic and of suggesting for pedagogical purposes some of the keys for a first reading.

1. *The New Bible and Dante's Mission*

As we all know, the *Divine Comedy* is a journey, like two earlier masterpieces, the *Odyssey* and the *Aeneid*. Dante never read the *Odyssey* in Greek, but he was familiar with the several references in Cicero and Statius, as well as with the Latin translation of its first two lines in Horace's *Ars Poetica* (141–42), and with Ovid's imaginative tale in Book XIV of the *Metamorphoses*. He knew the *Aeneid*, however, in its every detail (see *Inf.* XX.114). In the *Aeneid*, Vergil tells us that as Aeneas journeys to the underworld, meeting those condemned to eternal labor as well as the dead heroes of Troy and finally his own father, he reexplores his own social group, his own polis, and his own past, as a man and as a Trojan. It is, in fact, through the contact with this past that his strength is restored and he becomes able to continue with renewed vigor toward the fulfillment of his great mission. Dante is at once the new Ulysses and the new Aeneas. Like Ulysses he learns about people, about the city of man and the city of God. Like Aeneas, he travels because his journey is wanted by the powers of heaven; he also meets, if not his father, an ancestor, Cacciaguida, who predicts his future and gives him the mission of writing the poem; and, finally, he too has a guide—not the Sibyl, but Vergil himself, the greatest poet and sage that ever lived, the personification of human knowledge and human reason at their best. Writing his poem, then, is for Dante what founding Rome and creating a new civilization are for Aeneas.

The conception of life as a journey was a commonplace often repeated by the Fathers of the Church. Dante charged it with new significance in the *Divine Comedy* by representing human life as a pilgrimage from error to truth, from darkness to life, from isolation and alienation to complete association and communion. And like Aeneas', Dante's journey has a definite purpose established by God. We are told repeatedly that such a journey was decreed in heaven. In the *Paradiso* Dante even states that he is a mere scribe, one who records what he sees and hears, just like the authors of the Old and New Testaments, which were written under the inspiration of the divinity. It is in this context of the poem being the Bible of the new times, inspired by God, that we must read all the passages dealing with the predestined journey and with the great mission of Dante.

In his letter to Can Grande della Scala, Dante calls the *Divine Comedy* a "doctrinal" work—the word "doctrinal" encompassing in his text also the meaning and function of "didactical," at least in a general sense—a work intended to expound a specific doctrine and at the same time to teach us, singly and collectively, how to observe the human and divine laws and thus to constitute an ideal society. The doctrine is present both directly, as when Vergil pauses to impart his thoughts, and indirectly, through the striking scenes and the depictions of personages in the various divisions of his imaginary world. Dante had learned from the parables of the Gospel, the works of the Fathers of the Church, the sermons from contemporary pulpits, and all literature, ancient and modern, that ideas when accompanied by, or presented in the guise of, examples are far more effective than when stated directly. Thus the individuals the pilgrim meets during his journey are intended to tell us where certain actions lead, and thus to serve as examples of either good or evil.

Dante was convinced that to write an enduring poem it was not enough simply to create a flow of beautiful and artistic images: the poem also had to be beneficial to mankind. In his letter to Can Grande, he declared that the purpose of the poem was "to remove the living from a state of misery and to guide them to a state of happiness": in other words, the purpose of the *Divine Comedy* is exactly the same as the purpose of the scripture. Beatrice herself, the pilgrim's guide to the heights of the kingdom of God, firmly asserts this purpose at the top of the great mountain of purgatory. There, when Dante, having just drunk of the waters of Lethe, is free of all memories and, consequently, everything he sees or hears will be indelibly stamped on his mind, she turns to him to tell him that he is the chosen one. True, soon he will be with her, forever a citizen of the city of Christ, but first he has to fulfill a mission for the salvation of mankind:

> Però, in pro del mondo che mal vive,
> al carro tieni or li occhi, e quel che vedi,
> ritornato di là, a che tu scrive.

Thus, for the good of the world which lives in evil, keep your eyes on the cart, and, once you return to the other side, be sure you write what you see. (*Purg.* XXXII. 103–05; translations throughout are mine)

Here Beatrice, with the voice of God himself, peremptorily orders Dante to write the poem for the purpose of redeeming the world. Later, when Dante asks his great-great-great-grandfather if he should really report everything that he has seen and heard, including all the invectives against his contemporaries, Cacciaguida will answer: "Tutta tua vision fa manifesta" ("make your entire vision clearly known" [*Par.* XVII. 128]). And Saint Peter, after delivering a raging speech against the "rotten" pastors of the Church, turns to Dante, saying:

E tu, figliuol, che per lo mortal pondo
ancor giù tornerai, apri la bocca,
e non asconder quel ch'io non ascondo.

And you, my son, who, because of your mortal weight, will
return down again, open your mouth, and do not hide what I am
not hiding. (*Par.* XXVII. 64–66).

Finally, like the new Bible, ordained in heaven and written by divine inspiration for the salvation of mankind, the *Divine Comedy* com-
prehends, reinterprets, and transfigures all the knowledge that human
beings may need, exactly like a universal encyclopedia.

2. Dante's Moral System. What Is Sin?

In the Scholastic conception of the world, everything springs from,
and returns to, a center. The physical was created to be subordinated
to the spiritual, with ultimately only the spiritual remaining, on the
other side of the sphere of time, and with each one of the spirits being
either rewarded or punished according to the use they have made of
their ability to act. In this world each creature exists only in relation to
its creator, who has established a certain order, everyone belonging to
a group that lives by the rules of a certain hierarchy, according to
which the various members, through constant obedience and performance of specific duties, are organized in a pyramidal form, more or
less like the court of a king or of a tribal chief. Everything and
everyone has a function, and all functions one by one are interdependent, while all together they must constitute a harmonious chorus.
Consequently, the so-called Glory of the Lord corresponds to the general benefit of the social group, as well as of its individual components,
with the result of an ideal social order. This order can be broken and
shattered by the intrusion of evil, which in Dante, and in the Western
tradition as we know it, consists in "offending," that is to say, in
damaging others, by omission or commission, by action or by intention.
At the beginning of the poem, Vergil (the personification of human
reason) quotes Beatrice (the personification of divine knowledge) as
saying:

Temer si dee di sole quelle cose
c'hanno potenza di fare altrui male;
de l'altre no, ché non son paurose.

We must fear only those things that have the power of hurting
people; and not the others, which are not to be feared (*Inf.* II.
88–90).

Dante's world is organized according to this principle. Sin becomes graver and graver the more people it damages, beginning with the least serious offenses that hurt primarily the individual sinner and moving all the way down to the sin of treachery, which damages entire cities, entire nations, or even all of humankind, as in the cases of Judas, Brutus, and Cassius. Evil is the deliberate violation of one's commitment to others; therefore, those who are guilty of this violation by omission, such as homosexuals and suicides, must be punished as severely as those who are guilty by commission.

Dante's inferno is the realm of those who, having been injurious to others, have been separated from the social body. They are alienated and isolated; they scream each alone in a savage cacophony. In purgatory, on the other hand, we find a harmonious society in which everyone accepts responsibility for his or her own actions, deplores any damage inflicted on others, and behaves like an integral part of a group. Purgatory is a society as society might be on earth but is not, for the society on earth is actually much more like hell, where in fact the poet meets a great many of the Florentines of his day. And finally, in paradise, in the realm where the human being is pure spirit, without any remnants of selfish inclinations, we find that ideal society which is impossible to achieve on earth.

3. Dante's Politics and Theory of Government

The *Divine Comedy* is many things and can be read from many points of view, but first of all it is a political poem, the greatest work of political protest ever written. For Dante, men and women are political animals in the sense that they belong to a polis, or city, or community and must contribute actively to it. Political action and leadership are therefore some of the highest forms of moral, or immoral, activity.

The entire structure of the *Divine Comedy* is saturated with political remarks and invectives. It is as if Dante had written his great poem, and had brought into it both heaven and earth (see *Par.* XXV. 2), almost with the sole aim of denouncing the politics of the various states and cities of Europe, of condemning the popes, and of building a gigantic pedestal for his own theories of government, theories he had already discussed in his Latin work *De Monarchia* (*On Government*). Of course, Dante's constant and tenacious preoccupation with politics had profound roots.

Born into the nobility of Florence, Dante aspired and prepared himself to become one of the leaders of the city. He spent many years absorbing as much learning as possible: he studied all the poetic, philosophical, theological, and scientific works of the past. He fought for Florence; he joined the guild of physicians and apothecaries, served as a knight, as an ambassador, and as a magistrate. Dante's party fell from power, however, and he was condemned to pay a fine, to be banished from the city for two years, and to be forever excluded from public office. A few months later, the banishment was declared perpetual, and his lifelong exile began. To Dante, exile was one of the greatest calamities that could have befallen him. For the rest of his life he kept hoping to be readmitted to his beloved city. He temporarily joined a band of other exiles who made a futile attempt to return by force of arms; he wrote letters to the Florentines and to Henry VII of Luxembourg, asking him to reestablish his legitimate imperial rule over Italy. Later in life, when everything else had failed, he even proclaimed that the great poem he was about to complete should merit for him the laurel crown in the beautiful Baptistery of his native city (see *Par.* XXV. 1–9). But he was never allowed to return to Florence.

During those years of wandering he had ample opportunity to meditate on his own destiny and on the vicissitudes of states and governments. He had been the innocent victim of a political upheaval that he viewed as fraudulent. To him, this upheaval proved that there was something deeply corrupt in the world, which concerned not only Dante as an individual but the entire social structure and all contemporary governments. And since the one responsible was the pope, Dante became convinced that the Church hierarchy was at the root of all social evil.

I believe that it was primarily for the purpose of condemning the corruption of the contemporary political world and of suggesting possible remedies that Dante's compelling need to write the *Divine Comedy* was born. Had he not been condemned to exile and had he stayed in Florence instead, he probably would not have written the poem, or at least he would have written it in a completely different form. This speculation does not contradict Dante's ability in the *Divine Comedy* to concentrate on a vast philosophical and theological system and on a good deal of the history of the world and of the universe, as he understood them.

The journey of the *Divine Comedy* begins 8 April (or less probably 25 March) 1300, which was Good Friday, a day of meditation and profound sadness. Dante finds that he has strayed into a dark forest of error and vice, which undoubtedly refers to the corruption of his city. In fact, it was precisely in the spring of 1300 that he had become especially active in the political leadership of Florence, when he was sent on a mission to San Gemignano and elected a chief magistrate.

Obviously, then, the *Divine Comedy* has autobiographical roots, and its invectives against Florence sprout directly from these roots. But Dante, educated in Aristotle and the Scholastic philosophers, quickly overcomes the particular and turns it into the universal. For this reason his invectives are neither directly nor solely motivated by his own personal sufferings but are elicited by his vision of the cause of these sufferings: a society whose leaders have become corrupt. If grave injustices have been committed against him, Florence is at fault and not the other way around. The Florentines have been unjust toward many others as well, and they must therefore be condemned and urged to mend their ways. But Florence itself becomes a microcosmic image of a much larger human sphere, since for Dante the corruption of Florence results from the corruption of Italy (see *Purg.* VI. 76–151), and the corruption of Italy in turn results from the corruption of Europe and of the whole earth—"l'aiuola che ci fa tanto feroci" ("the little yard that makes us so ferocious" [*Par.* XXII. 151]). The poem, then, is constructed in such a way as to define the reasons for denouncing the deplorable conditions of human society: from the cantos leading to *Inferno* VI and *Purgatorio* VI to all the invectives against the political leaders, the Roman Curia, and the popes, and finally to Beatrice's last fiery condemnation of nepotist popes in *Paradiso* XXX. 142–48.

Like Machiavelli two centuries later, Dante believed that we are selfish and greedy and that greed is the root of all evil, for to satisfy it, we lose all scruples. Modern society, Dante insists, was led astray by the greed of its leaders, who were mainly clerical people on all levels of the Church hierarchy, including the pope. According to Dante, only one recent pope, Celestine V, might have been just and saintly, but he had abdicated. That greed for riches is the root of all evil is first and foremost demonstrated by the transformations of the cart in *Purgatorio* XXXII. 124–69, where, as a result of the Donation of Constantine, the "holy building" becomes a hideous monster. Such a Donation was allegedly the gift of the Western Roman Empire to Pope Sylvester; Dante, a man of the Middle Ages, never questioned its authenticity.

But as he meditated on the so-called Donation of Constantine in the light of the evangelical precept "Render unto Caesar what is Caesar's and render unto God what is God's" and as he tried to envision a cure for the widespread decadence of the Church and of society in general, he came to the conclusion that the Donation itself had been illegal. Starting from this premise, he wrote *De Monarchia* (*On Government*) to demonstrate that only a lay government was acceptable to human society for secular affairs, while the activities of the Church were to be restricted to the mission of guiding human beings toward eternal salvation.

In the center of the *Divine Comedy,* Dante introduces a wise man, Marco Lombardo, who supposedly is experienced in government and courts but in actuality is Dante's other self. Dante asks him who is to blame for humankind's straying from the right path; Marco Lombardo immediately answers that the leadership is at fault. In his brief but extremely significant speech, Marco Lombardo casts aside the old papal theory whereby the pope is symbolized by the sun, while the emperor is viewed as the moon, for he supposedly receives light, or guidance, from the sun. Dante declares that pope and emperor are separate and equal; then he explains that without the separation of Church and State there cannot be any checks or balances; the result is that corruption is unavoidable. The significance and the far-reaching ramifications of this theory of government require no comment.

Dante touches on the fundamental importance of both Church and State in organized society in many different contexts. One of the most interesting occurs at the end of the *Inferno,* where, as already noted, Judas, who had betrayed the founder of the Church, and Brutus and Cassius, who had betrayed the one who had been (at least symbolically) the founder of the Empire, that is, organized society, are forever devoured in Lucifer's three mouths. Another occurs at the top of paradise, in the already quoted episode of Beatrice's last speech, in which, before condemning the pope's blind greed, she points at the throne of Henry VII, who "will come to straighten out Italy, before it is ready" (see *Par.* XXX. 137–38).

We may add that at the end of his poem, when Dante points at the high goal of the human pilgrimage, he is rejoicing in his own personal salvation, he knows that he has expressed his social and political opinions and that he has said enough to help mankind back onto the right path, but he also seems to be telling us that he finally is, and wants to remain, far above all that political and social misery that is being fostered by greedy and irresponsible leaders.

4. Invention of Punishments

From the beginning, Dante's journey suggests that men and women were created to live in harmonious association with one other and that therefore hell consists in disassociation or alienation. As a result, evil is imbued with a gravity of its own, pulling the sinner down toward that sad pit to which everything gravitates (see *Inf.* XXXII. 2–3).

For Dante, all punishments in the *Inferno* and the *Purgatorio* obey the law of *contrapasso* (*Inf.* XXVIII. 142), or retribution, for according to the Scholastic philosophers, who had derived the concept from Aristotle, one must pay for a transgression with a punishment of the same nature as the transgression itself. In reality, Dante invents the various punishments by following a simple rule: he takes common metaphors and translates them into concrete, visual events, even to the point of extracting some of those metaphors from the etymology of words: the lustful, who forgot all the duties and let themselves be carried away by the tempest of the senses, are placed inside a real storm; the gluttons, who "made pigs" of themselves, lie in the mire; those who spilled the blood of others are submerged in rivers of boiling blood; the soothsayers are condemned to look backward; the evil counselors are clothed in tongues of fire; those who split up social groups are constantly sawed through so that their limbs are also split up; those who were gnawed by envy (from the Latin verb *invideo*, "to see against") have their eyes sewn up, and so forth.

Hell has a general cathartic function for both the protagonist and humankind in general. In purgatory, which is structured on the basis of the confession, or the acceptance of responsibility for one's mistakes, Dante is at once the spectator of the state of those who live in hope and the coparticipant in their process of purification.

5. Statius: The Nobility and Redeeming Power of Poetry

In the *Purgatorio* Dante addresses with considerable insistence one of the things that interest him most: poetry. His conception of poetry is high. For him, the poet is also a prophet, the innately noble custodian of perennial wisdom who can do no wrong. For this reason he chooses an ancient poet as his guide toward salvation. With the single exception of Bertran de Born, whom Dante does not seem to consider especially great, no poet is in hell proper. The ancient ones, from Homer to Ovid to Lucan, are in a privileged area of Limbo; the more modern ones are in purgatory, in the company of those who will ascend to paradise. Poets cannot be damned, for they understand the needs, destiny, and nature of each human being; their minds are enlightened, and therefore they cannot be possessed by error, which is synonymous with evil.

It is especially significant that when Dante wishes to discuss how a soul leaves purgatory to ascend to paradise, he chooses as his example

Statius, a poet, rather than a hero, a saint, or a political leader. Statius explains that he was famous in Rome during the reign of Emperor Titus "col nome che più dura e che più onora" ("with the name that endures most and honors most" [*Purg.* XXI. 85]). This is clearly a definition of "poet," a definition to which Statius soon will try to add by calling his spirit "vocal." It is a remarkable definition not only because with it Dante states, or at least implies, that the poet is immortal just because he is a poet but also because of the circumstances under which it is pronounced: Statius is supposed to be completely purified of earthly inclinations, totally detached from the *vanitas vanitatum* of human glory, exclusively guided by an intense desire to be admitted to the presence of God for eternity. Yet, he pronounces words of extraordinarily high praise for the "vocal spirit" of a poet (hence, of himself) on earth. Obviously, Dante considers poetry so great an achievement that in front of it he momentarily ignores even the firm theological foundations of his poem.

Statius elaborates on his definition. He could not complete the second of his complex narrative poems, but whatever he did was due only to the inspiration of the *Aeneid*; and in this manner he declares that the great works of poetry are all interconnected and interdependent, like human generations. But Vergil, and therefore poetry, was responsible not only for the excellence of Statius' works but also for his conversion to Christianity and for his salvation as well. In the beginning of his *Fourth Eclogue* (5–7), Vergil had celebrated a "new order of centuries," a new golden age, which was about to begin with "a new son coming down from heaven." Statius says that this particular passage (which in the Middle Ages was generally interpreted as referring to the coming of Christ) convinced him to embrace Christianity and thus achieve salvation.

Through Statius' exaltation of the *Aeneid*, of Vergil, and of poets in general, Dante actually praises his own noble mind and establishes the mission of his own poem. As Vergil's words had led Statius to salvation, so Dante's own words should save humankind from the abyss of perdition. In the whole Statius episode we can read a statement of what Dante himself believes his own poetry should be and do. Vergil is the master from whom he too has derived his "style"; now he expects that this style, in all the possible meanings of the term, will have the same effect on men and women as Vergil's original style had on Statius. Thus, as the highest of human activities, poetry is viewed as capable of redeeming all of humankind. In this sense, Dante's mission is far greater than Vergil's.

6. *Experience and Process of Learning: Paradise Is Complete Knowledge*

While the *Divine Comedy* is a celebration of poetry, it is also the glorification of knowledge, for only knowledge can free us from error (that is to say, from sin and damnation) and can lead us to truth, the equivalent of salvation. Vergil characterizes the damned as those "c'hanno perduto il ben de l'intelletto" ("who have lost the good of the intellect" [*Inf.* III. 18]), in short, those who have lost the truth. Their torment is to feel forever the excruciating need for what they cannot have. It might be said that the torture of hell consists in continuous and profound frustration, since men and women were born "per seguir virtute e canoscenza" ("to pursue noble deeds and knowledge" [*Inf.* XXVI. 120]), and since there cannot be noble deeds without knowledge. This lofty conception of the meaning of life and of the destiny of humankind is the basis of the entire *Divine Comedy*. The minds of the spirits in hell are permanently obfuscated; in purgatory the spirits are gradually becoming enlightened; and in paradise they have reached complete happiness by sharing in total knowledge with the Omniscient.

According to the *Divine Comedy*, we are born with an intense desire for knowledge, a "sete natural" ("natural thirst" [*Purg.* XXI. 1]), which can be quenched only by absorbing, and being absorbed by, the truth. It is mainly to satisfy this thirst for truth that Dante the protagonist keeps questioning his guides, Vergil and Beatrice. His journey is an unceasing and progressive acquisition of knowledge (and so, incidentally, is the reader's journey). Whatever he learns, and whatever human beings learn, is called "experience." In fact, in the *Divine Comedy esperienza* ("experience") refers to the knowledge that is acquired to satisfy the natural need that now is sometimes defined as intellectual curiosity. This is the meaning of the word as we encounter it on Ulysses' lips: "Non vogliate negar l'esperienza, / di retro al sol, del mondo sanza gente" ("do not deny [your brief lives] the experience of the world without people, following the sun's path" [*Inf.* XXVI. 116–17]). Knowledge per se will not always lead to salvation, as Ulysses demonstrates, but the knowledge that both the traveler Dante and the reader acquire as they move on will most certainly help them; it will have both a cathartic and an enriching function.

If salvation coincides with the full satisfaction of the intellect, with knowing everything there is to know, paradise is clearly the place where such a condition can finally be achieved. Dante's is the traditional Christian paradise, but its conceptual roots are discernible in the culture and civilization of ancient Greece. It is, in fact, in the poetic and philosophical texts of ancient Greece that the innate thirst for knowledge is recognized and encouraged. It was in that period that intelligence was deified in Athena and poetry exalted in Apollo, and storytellers recorded the myth of Odysseus, the one who knew everything about the customs of the people and cities of the world. It was during that period that the great philosophers lived, in particular Aristotle, who represents the greatest personification of our unceasing search for knowledge and who is for Dante "maestro di color che sanno" ("master of those who know" [*Inf.* IV. 131]).

Christian theology acknowledges this human compulsion to know everything and at the same time realistically admits the impossibility of satisfying it because too much escapes our limited intellect: a finite mind cannot comprehend the infinite, except when it is strengthened beyond all human confines. Consequently, only before the Omniscient and sharing in his possession of all knowledge, can we learn everything and quench our perennial thirst. This is the Christian, and Dantesque conception of paradise, which is totally pervaded by the intense light of truth and knowledge the same way that hell is submerged into the darkness of error and ignorance.

7. The Visual Imagination

In the *Divine Comedy, esperienza* chiefly coincides with the actual visual contacts with the specific phenomena of the other world, those phenomena that the writer creates and the protagonist perceives. There can be no question that Dante translates nearly everything into visual images, not only the clumsy bulkiness of hell but also the joyous bliss of paradise and even God himself under the mysterious semblance of the Trinity. But this is apparent to the reader on the surface. Dante, just like any other poet, projects his own perceptions and sensations, or the memory of those perceptions and sensations, while he attempts to evoke another world. What he sees is the result of a mixture of visual perceptions and imagination. Because of this incessant process of synthesis, Dante creates, and the protagonist experiences, a new world, absorbs it, and translates it into the substance of his own self. Throughout the journey Dante says, "Vidi" ("I saw"), an almost uncountable number of times. The words *vedere* ("to see"), *occhi* ("eyes"), *viso* ("eyesight"), and *vista* ("sight") are by far the most recurrent expressive units of the entire poem; the forms of the verb *vedere* alone occur approximately eight hundred times, or an average of eight times per canto.

Through his images, Dante transmits his own personal history. The triple-faced Lucifer, for example, is a figure Dante must have seen in a more rudimentary form in the mosaics of the Baptistery of Florence. But Dante also relives and transfigures all the human experience, of the past as well as of the present. In fact, as we read the *Divine Comedy*, we watch Dante see and contemplate, but at the same time we rediscover the images and perceptions of our own past. Already the mention of the "dark wood" of the second line brings back to us seemingly long-lost sensations, far and beyond the allegorical significance, charging the old image in the new context. Proceeding from the first lines of the *Inferno*, we encounter an extraordinary number of impressions that evoke specific moments of our past, from the flowers straightening up in the morning (*Inf.* II. 127–29) to the leaves abandoning the trees in the fall (*Inf.* III. 112–14), the fresh brand that whistles as it burns (*Inf.* XIII. 40–42), the flame moving back and forth on a greasy surface (*Inf.* XIX. 28–29), the fireflies filling the valley with silent sparks (*Inf.* XXVI. 25–30), and so on. Were we to mention all the fresh images of the *Divine Comedy*, including those contained in single words, not only would we find ourselves transcribing most of the poem, but we would triple or quadruple the impressions and the fleeting visions the years have stored up inside us. Like the few other great poets of humankind, Dante is capable of enriching even the details of our own personal history.

It would be fascinating to ascertain how certain images that have clung to the depths of a person's mind from childhood—like the figure of the flowers, for instance—are suddenly revitalized to travel with him or her from the beginning of the *Inferno* to the end of the *Purgatorio* (cf. XXVII. 36–42) and the end of the *Paradiso* (cf. XXX. 61–66), where those flowers become the visual counterparts of invisible substances. Through this process of transfiguration Dante transforms his own (and our) experience into perennial figures. In this sense the *Paradiso*, as the realm in which the purely spiritual is unceasingly transposed into the perceptible forms of human experience, must be considered the greatest poetic achievement in history. There the poet invents figures of all kinds—a gigantic cross, a series of letters, an eagle consisting of thousands of souls speaking in perfect unison, a river of light flanked by banks of flowers, and so on—which make visible the invisible. From the time our protagonist sets his foot on the moon to the time he contemplates the entire universe bound up in one volume, and finally to the time he rejoices in the profound bliss of full knowledge, the poem is the astonishing sensible display of a "high," almost superhuman, "imagination" (see *Par.* XXXIII. 142).

8. The Creation of a Language

If the *Divine Comedy* was to be the great book of knowledge, the sacred book for the salvation of humankind, intended to reach everyone, it had to be written in a language that was accessible and understandable, and not in Latin, the idiom of the learned, which was already remote from the expressive habits of the people. Dante states this criterion plainly in his letter to Can Grande, in which he refers to a "lowly" and "humble" language. Indeed, the entire gamut of Florentine popular speech seems to have entered the poem, with its recognizable inflections and tones. The very first lines, "Nel mezzo del cammin di nostra vita / mi ritrovai per una selva oscura" ("Midway in the journey of our life, I found myself in a dark wood"), are imbued with the cadence of the popular speech. Anyone walking the streets of Florence at the time of Dante could have heard exactly the same words with the same cadence, as anyone could hear them now. Even the verb *mi ritrovai*, in the meaning of "I found (or discovered) myself," was, and still is, a current local expression. We might be tempted to go so far as to say that the whole poem is written in this intonation, but the truth is that Dante was thoroughly acquainted with the expressive patterns of a long literary tradition and was able to assimilate them and to apply them to this new medium.

It has often been said that Dante is the father of the Italian language—an observation that is undoubtedly accurate. To transform the Florentine dialect (and the Tuscan dialect in general) into a powerful poetic instrument, he used all the words available, invented others, and derived still others from Latin. Since in the fourteenth century philosophical and theological matters were discussed only in Latin, Dante italianized the necessary words for discussion of philosophy and theology, such as *continga, contingenza* ("contingency"), and many others. These words have remained in the Italian language and have even passed into other European languages.

But it is particularly important to keep in mind that, since words contain images, by extending the vocabulary of the common language Dante also amplifies his potential for creating images. As we have seen, his personal experience generally derives both from direct action and perception and from the numerous books he has assimilated. But to express all the areas of human experience he has absorbed, he needs a varied and rich language. Yet even simply adapting a word or inventing another by remolding and extending certain everyday sounds means creating completely new sounds and new flavors, and, consequently, giving our speech a very special tonality, which the speaker (author) is the first to hear. I often wonder how Dante must have tasted certain words (*rime aspre e chiocce, tristo buco* [*Inf.* XXXII. 1–2], *trasumanar* [*Par.* I. 70], *ingigliarsi* [*Par.* XVIII. 13], *inluiarsi* [*Par.* IX. 73], etc.), at the very moment he pronounced them and then heard them echo in his mind. It must have been a constantly new experience in vision and sound, a *visibile parlare* ("visible speech" [*Purg.* X. 95]), if we want to recall Dante's own definition of the artist's ability to transform even sounds into visual patterns. The same must be said of the many words that Dante derived from Latin and rendered, in a certain sense, definitive. Once they were italianized, they acquired new sound implications, new suggestive associations with already existing words. Now, after they have been routinely pronounced for so many centuries, we find it difficult to perceive even a small portion of the vibrations they must have contained and deposited on the lips that uttered them for the first time. So much less can we imagine what a man of Dante's sensitivity must have felt as he pronounced them for the first time, not as terms of general significance, but as an integral part of his own personal expressive patterns and of his life.

Even if seen from a statistical viewpoint, the *Divine Comedy* encompasses a very large sphere of expressive forms. Its vocabulary is by far richer than that of any literary work that preceded it. From the first to the last line, the language accompanies the traveler, adapting itself to a vast range of situations from the horrible to the sublime; in fact, it *is* those situations. The poet often interrupts the narrative to tell the reader that his expressive level must change to fit the subject matter. Thus, at the end of the *Inferno* he says he wishes he had much harsher-sounding words to be able to portray the hole toward which all evil gravitates (*Inf.* XXXII. 1–15); in the *Purgatorio* as the traveler is about to enter the realm of the saved, Dante tells us not to be surprised if, together with the subject matter, he must also raise his style and the quality of his words (*Purg.* IX. 70–72); and in the *Paradiso* he proudly states that he is now sailing in uncharted seas, where both the subject matter and the expressive forms will be very difficult to grasp, so exalted and so far removed from the normal world of human perceptions and communication are they (*Par.* II. 1–9).

9. *The Two Dantes: Poet and Protagonist*

I cannot conclude without first briefly discussing the question of the differentiation of the two Dantes in the *Divine Comedy:* the poet and the protagonist. As we read the poem and participate in its great adventure, we feel many times that the traveler is a human entity other than the poet, that he may be defined as the poet's other self, the self that Dante sends on a journey to gain full experience, thereby to achieve rebirth and redemption through complete mastery of himself, while the poet watches him closely to record whatever he does and thinks. Yet such a dichotomy between the two cannot be excessively sharp, even if some recent scholars tend to preclude any possibility for their meeting and merging into one.

As a matter of fact, it cannot be denied that the protagonist and the poet do overlap continually. It would be very difficult, for instance, to attribute only to the protagonist such passages as the invocation to the spirit of poetry (the Muses or Apollo), the many comments related to the expressive patterns called for by the specific circumstances and to the poem per se, such as the comment on the structure of the canticle at the end of the *Purgatorio* (XXXIII. 139–41), the remark to Cacciaguida about acquiring fame among future generations (*Par.* XVII. 120), the definition of the poem as "sacred" in *Paradiso* XXV. 1, and Dante's hope to be called back to Florence and crowned a poet on the font of his baptism (*Par.* XXV. 1–9). The same holds true for all those points in which Dante speaks about poetry, his own as well as that of his ancestors, as in *Purgatorio* XXIV and XXVI, the invectives against the popes in *Inferno* XIX, or the tirades against Italy in *Purgatorio* VI. It is unquestionable that there are many instances in the poem when Dante the poet and Dante the protagonist are one and the same person.

It is also unquestionable that the direct presence of the poet is somewhat sporadic and that it is the protagonist who has to experience the three realms of the other world. This protagonist does exist. It must be kept in mind, however, that he always carries with him the many visual and aural memories that belong to the poet and that at times cause him to speak with the poet's lips. Thus we might say that it is through this other self that the poet relives for us the perceptions and observations he has kept in store during a long period of years. As the protagonist acquires new knowledge in this process of learning, so does the poet. When the last line of the poem is down on paper, the supreme bliss of paradise, which consists in abandoning oneself to the flow of total knowledge, has been achieved by the protagonist, and by the poet, who finally lays down his pen.

The two Dantes, then, reflect the process of learning not only on the part of our poet, but on the part of humankind in general. The *Divine Comedy* demonstrates for the first time that each one of us is actually two people: the one who acts almost instinctively, thereby going through the most unexpected adventures and slowly learning the true values of life, and the one who observes and reflects on what the other is doing.

Here I must acknowledge that while in the preceding pages I have discussed many different topics, all related to Dante's *Divine Comedy*, I have left many others untouched, such as, for example, the very prominent place philosophy and theology have in the poem. Philosophy and theology must be viewed as an indispensable and obvious support for any poem dealing with the three Christian realms of the other world. Yet they have little to do with poetry or with artistic achievement. If philosophy and theology were to be considered the substance of poetry, Thomas Aquinas, and not Dante, would be the greatest poet of the Middle Ages. For us, they only constitute the framework within whose confines Dante's "alta fantasia" ("high imagination" [*Par.* XXXII. 142]) freely moved. Students will find all they need in this area by consulting one of the many commentaries available. Meanwhile, it is hoped that they can glean some other insights from these pages, which were optimistically intended to underline a few of the aspects of the *Divine Comedy* that are often neglected by scholars, commentators, and teachers.

PHILOSOPHIES OF TEACHING AND READING THE *DIVINE COMEDY*

DANTE'S *DIVINE COMEDY*: DRAMA AS TEACHING

~ for Francis Fergusson ~

Glauco Cambon

Few teachers would deny that, of the towering masterpieces of Western literature, Dante's *Divine Comedy* is the most difficult to negotiate for most undergraduate college students. Even in his native Italy, where the official language is still recognizably the one Dante used, the *Divine Comedy* proves far from easy for the average class, if only because of the thick historical references, which the author had every reason to take for granted in his time but which the modern reader can hardly grasp without the help of a massive footnote apparatus that can itself become a forbidding visual barrier on the printed page. Even more discouraging, Dante's commitment to the specifics of Scholastic thought threatens to isolate much of his writing from a readership largely used to less demanding intellectual fare.

It is ironic that Dante's didactic intention should be frustrated by the very doctrine he hoped to teach. The *Divine Comedy* had few readers outside Italy in the Renaissance and the Enlightenment, and the eager interpreters it attracted during its romantic revival (especially De Sanctis, and Croce later) tended to dismiss its doctrinal scaffolding for the sake of its recurrent dramatic immediacy. Nevertheless, that seemingly arbitrary surgical strategy (heresy to modern defenders of the structural unity and doctrinal implications of the poem, such as Singleton, Brandeis, or Freccero) helped generations of readers to venture into the dark (or dazzling) wood of the *Divine Comedy* with the assurance that they would find poetry there, the true incentive and goal of their initiation into medieval lore.

This concentration on the poetry and drama is something that today's teacher might want to remember. Even those students who, lacking a working knowledge of Italian, have to miss the unique music Dante extracted from his language, can respond to the power of fable, to the narrative skill, sustained by vivid imagery, that survives translation; there is no lack of perspicuous translations, notably those of Thomas G. Bergin and Charles S. Singleton. My teaching experience tells me that such emphasis will make the students' journey into the depths and heights of the *Divine Comedy* a truly rewarding adventure of the mind. But the instructor must be prepared to become to his or her students what Vergil is to Dante, the character in the story that Dante the poet has written for us. Lest anyone object that this is too much to ask, I beg to point out that Vergil, the exalted poet and savant, actually functions in the poem as the wise, but by no means infallible, teacher. If none of us modern teachers can hope to match Vergil's exceptional competence in matters of the nether world, or in literary accomplishment, we can certainly understand his occasional bewilderment at puzzling and threatening situations from which only divine intervention can extricate him and his frustration at his all-too-human charge; we should have no trouble identifying with the affection he bestows on his troublesome pupil.

In a poem that focuses on the (re)education of an errant person, on the "(re)growth of a poet's mind" from confusion to clarity—that is, on the perennial drama of learning—the complementary process of teaching is bound to receive commensurate emphasis, as indeed happens in the *Divine Comedy* through the agency of characters like Vergil, Brunetto Latini, Statius, and eventually Beatrice. Of them all, Vergil most memorably embodies the teaching function vis-à-vis Dante, the traveler who will return from the as yet "undiscovered country," the groping wanderer bound for vatic initiation at the hands of the ancient Roman poet and the saintly Tuscan lady who takes over at the top of Mount Purgatory. And if we single out this thematic strand from the several that interweave in the poem's structure, we will gain both as readers of the inexhaustible poem and as instructors who try to make it more accessible to those who are younger and less-trained readers than we.

The teacher-pupil twosome, Vergil and Dante, has attained mythic life in the memory of the West along with such other literary couples as

Don Quixote and Sancho Panza, King Lear and his fool, Faust and Mephistopheles, Prince Myshkin and Rogozhin. This status the two Dantesque characters owe to their author's uncanny imagination, for Dante has endowed them, through their shared pilgrim's progress, with those individualizing traits that bring them both to dramatic life, each by himself as well as in their archetypal bond. The shrewd teacher will refrain from overemphasizing the poem's abstract allegorical meanings (Vergil as Human Reason, Dante as Everyman, the dark wood as Sin and Error, etc.) and will draw attention instead to the imaginative particulars that enable readers to apprehend each fictional gesture and scene and the overall situation, the developing rapport between teacher and learner in Dante's complex poem, as something concretely significant.

Viewed accordingly, the poem has the power to make learners and teachers of us. Just as Dante learns to interpret his extraordinary experience, morally and intellectually, with Vergil's expert assistance, for the benefit of those largely posthumous readers whom the poet hopes to reach, we gradually learn to decipher the poem's signs and then to share our knowledge with others. If we mind the clues, we can learn to be better teachers in the very act of becoming better readers. The two functions converge in us, beyond the text, in the communal space the poem intends to establish for its readers, both teachers and students.

Watching Vergil as a teacher in action is more than just listening with compunction to his eloquent tirades on the geography of hell (*Inf.* XI) or on the psychology and moral effects of love (*Purg.* XVII–XVIII). Many readers today are unwilling to be lectured, and their impatience would be justified if lectures were all that Vergil had to give. But he has more to offer, and his lectures themselves are timed to fit the pupil's schedule in judicious alternation with what I should like to call practical lessons. An authority on hell, Vergil imparts his knowledge to Dante the pilgrim at appropriate moments—to map out the trip, to survey the ground already covered, to anticipate the ground ahead—so that Dante may progressively orient himself. The lectures are not just informative, however; they also contribute to the dramatic movement, as when Vergil persuades Dante to follow him into hell (*Inf.* II), or when he gives the Florentine disciple a classical pep talk to spur him on up the backbreaking escarpments of Malebolge (*Inf.* XXIV. 46–57), or again when he rebukes Dante for indulging as viewer in the degrading wrangle between Sinon and Master Adam (*Inf.* XXX. 131–32). In such scenes word is action; it is rhetoric not in the demeaning sense our age generally gives to the term but in the long classical and medieval tradition that canonized rhetoric as the responsible use of language.

As I intimated above, however, Vergil's teaching skill exceeds his honest eloquence and also includes his resourceful behavioral tactics. After all, Vergil was engaged in field work rather than classroom education. For instance, when he introduces the still-uninitiated pilgrim to the storm-tossed souls of the second circle of hell, after succinctly describing the nature of their sin, he lets Dante take in the breathtaking scene, giving his pupil fruitful advice when he expresses an interest in talking to one particular couple of lost souls in the whirlwind: "See when they come closer; you then entreat them in the name of the love that leads them, and they will approach" (*Inf.* V. 76–78; my translation). What follows is one of the high points in the whole poem: Francesca tells her excruciating story in haunting verse, and Dante barely manages to control his sympathetic response. Vergil notices Dante's speechlessness, and he interjects a pointed question: "What are you thinking?" That one question suffices to help Dante over his psychological impasse; the pupil now addresses Francesca again, this time in the language of pity and passion she understands, thereby eliciting the final revelation that sinks in, irresistibly, to make Dante swoon and thus prepares him for the moral lesson to be drawn from this potentially destructive experience, which can only be called vicarious if one forgets that Dante himself had been much tormented by Eros. Not before the middle of purgatory will Vergil lecture his pupil on the nature and workings of love-libido, for only then will Dante be ready for such a rational approach; now he can only be accessible to empathy, for he is still comparatively unenlightened, almost as much so as the doomed souls who "submitted reason to instinct," and only this kind of psychological homeopathy can begin to reeducate him. Clearly, Vergil knows when to take the podium and when to stay in the background, and he wants his disciple to face each experience on his own, albeit under discreet guidance. In this way Dante relearns the quality of an experience instead of just accepting a preliminary explanation from an authoritative source. Rather than constantly leading him by the hand, solicitous Vergil applies a daring pedagogy: he lets Dante (to use Joseph Conrad's words from *Lord Jim*) immerse himself "in the destructive element" when necessary. This is a teacher "acquainted with the night," and he can hardly be accused of being overly protective.

The same self-effacing tact shows in the circle of the heretics when Vergil rescues Dante from another embarrassment by urging him to face up to the formidable warrior Farinata degli Uberti, who has just interrupted their conversation. What ensues after Vergil has pushed his shocked pupil toward the giant torso erect in the flaming tomb belongs to the most dramatic passages in world literature, for here Dante confronts his city's heritage, the sins of the fathers, and the unhealed lacerations that reach into his personal life. Old battles are fought again, old family wounds are reopened, and this searing therapy takes place at the prompting of Vergil, who by his energetic action impels Dante to meet the cruel memories of his tribe, the hopeless past and the seemingly hopeless present—Florence like Europe of World War II, Florence like Beirut of the 1970s, a divided house. Will the divided soul find reconciliation? Vergil keeps his peace throughout the impassioned exchange; he has simply acted as the catalyst.

And the limits of Vergil's power are also displayed clearly, as when he requires the intervention of a messenger from heaven to open the formidable gates of the city of Dis (*Inf.* IX). And Vergil's word does not always prevail on the wayward demons that repeatedly try to block Dante's progress. In Malebolge Vergil actually suffers mockery and deceit at the hands of the devils who pretend to show him the way. And in purgatory, a region physically if not morally new to him, he is often helpless or disoriented, as when he has to take Cato's curt rejoinder to an elaborate diplomatic entreaty in Canto I, or when he must ask the penitent souls for directions. Far from detracting from his stature, these incidents endear him to us, and his action in seeing Dante through the dangerous pilgrimage becomes that much more valuable. Needless to say, this uncertainty also contributes to dramatic suspense, for in purgatory the increasingly emancipated Dante and the less secure Vergil must share the perplexities of difficult progress.

Vergil's limits are those of a rationally and imaginatively developed man (and of the classical civilization he so fully represents): they do not diminish him; they define him. It is because of them that he can be such a convincing character and effective teacher. With Dante we remember his hesitations, his strong gestures and rebukes; with Dante we acutely miss him when, after bestowing on his pupil the crown of attained maturity and freedom in the Garden of Eden (*Purg.* XXVII), he discreetly disappears while Dante talks to the supervening Beatrice. Vergil's mission is fulfilled and he vanishes from the scene, as teachers and fathers are wont to do in real life, as Dante reiterates his name like a crying orphan (*Purg.* XXX. 46–55). But he hardly vanishes from our memory. Who could forget, for instance, Vergil's calculated shock tactics in the wood of the suicides, when he encourages his bewildered charge to break off one twig from a bush, with the result that the bush bleeds and cries in pain? Since the tree encloses the soul of the suicidal Pier delle Vigne, the gesture occasions a momentous dialogue between the former minister of Emperor Frederick II and Dante, who is eager to learn the dark lesson so that he may regain the light. Vergil then explains his educational motive to Dante. He wants to expose Dante to full experience before aiding him to account for it in rational terms.

In all, Vergil is the embodiment of reason in its heuristic, tentative, experience-bound aspect, not just the syllogistic. But Vergil is also a poet, and that makes him the better teacher. Doesn't this remind us that we must seek to use the poet in ourselves if we hope to bring our students of literature very close to that "delectable mountain," which, as the realm of poetry, is "the source and cause of all joy" (*Inf.* I. 77–78; my translation)? Imagination is the better part of understanding, and of teaching as well.

DANTE'S UNFOLDING VISION

Richard H. Lansing

> Dante does not explain hell . . .
> Philip Wicksteed

> The *experience* of poetry which this *Comedy* holds potentially
> . . . is precisely the experience of a gradual revelation of mean-
> ing, an *unveiling* (which happens to be the literal meaning of
> *revelatio*). Emerging meanings build on to what has gone be-
> fore, and when this happens, *then* it is the commentator's duty to
> note it, but not before.
> Charles Singleton

Philip Wicksteed's observation, which for convenience we may expand to embrace as well the other two realms of the afterlife, is a
statement of fact about the nature of Dante's poem. Charles Singleton's remark, appended to the commentary that accompanies his translation of the *Inferno,* is a rephrasing of the same observation from
another perspective. If Dante did not explain hell—characters, events,
and phenomena—it seemed to Singleton that neither should the com-
mentator, at least not until the proper moment. To do so would be to
violate the primacy of the poem's experience, or, to adopt the poem's
major metaphor, to transport its readers directly to the poem's destina-
tion and thereby deprive them of the experience of the journey. Dante
does not "explain" hell, purgatory, or paradise; they explain themselves, gradually, progressively, moment by moment. The fullness of
their meaning is ultimately accessible only on completion of a reading
of the entire poem. While this proposition may seem self-evident and
almost tautological, tantamount to saying that one cannot understand
the story until one has reached the climax, it nevertheless captures a
peculiar quality of the *Divine Comedy* that makes a reading of the
poem so much like the living of life itself. The poem unfolds its meanings gradually and accomplishes Dante's purpose principally by oblig-

61

ing the reader to accompany the pilgrim Dante on his journey through the otherworld, from his point of departure in the "selva oscura" in this world to his ascent in the "rosa mistica" in the Empyrean. The poem is a learning experience, a process of acquiring knowledge, of perfecting the self, of expanding moral consciousness, and as such it reflects the process of growth in the enlightened life. Put another way, the reader's progress coincides with the pilgrim's progress.

Wicksteed and Singleton stress the point that Dante's poem dramatizes the acquisition of knowledge by means of a progressive revelation of truth through experience and doctrine. There is of course a radical sense in which both of their statements are not true, or true only in a limited sense. Wicksteed would certainly not deny that Dante does some explaining when he gives us a map of the structure of hell in *Inferno* XI, or when he has Vergil explain the nature of love in *Purgatorio* XVII, or Beatrice the locus of the souls' true residence in the Empyrean in *Paradiso* IV. Nor would Singleton be likely to disagree with the fact that his statement describes the nature of a good number of other narratives; the habit of narrative is to defer final meaning until the end, and to make each moment in the narrative a stage in the development of its ultimate meaning. Nevertheless, both Wicksteed and Singleton have addressed themselves from different perspectives to a central truth about the *Divine Comedy* that is difficult to put another way. The poem is not a philosophical or ethical treatise but an imaginative vision, not a dry lecture but a vivid drama, not a sermon but a revelation. Dante does not explain the afterlife, interpret its meaning for us; rather, he places us on the scene in hell, purgatory, and paradise, so that we may discover rather than be told the essence of good and evil. If there are explanations voiced by Vergil, Beatrice, and others, they come generally by way of confirmation of an experience previously felt or in response to observed phenomena. Singleton demurs on explaining hell, for he knows that its fullest explanation lies in a reading of purgatory and paradise and that that experience comes later and must be deferred until the proper moment.

While the teacher of so notoriously complex and difficult a poem as the *Divine Comedy* can scarcely retreat from engaging in a good deal of explanation, commentary, and interpretation, it is important to preserve the primacy of the reader's experience of the text as a process that takes place through time and to emphasize the manner in which the pilgrim absorbs knowledge. This is one of my concerns in teaching the poem. I stress that how the poem discloses meaning to the reader is analogous to how the vision of the afterlife reveals its truths to the pilgrim, and that the *how* of disclosure and the *order* of disclosure are no less important than *what* is disclosed.

Dante's strategy of progressive revelation in the book of his poem is significant because he is imitating what he believes is God's way of revealing truth through the book of nature. Just as God's physical universe is an ordered system of signs, hieroglyphics, secret clues all pointing beyond themselves to a higher, invisible, transcendental reality of eternal truths, so Dante's poem is an ordered system of signs and images pointing beyond themselves to ideas whose meaning, because it is not explained by the poet, must be interpreted.

To learn how to interpret those signs requires a general familiarity with the historical age and cultural tradition in which Dante lived and which make up so much of the substance of his poem. Perhaps the single most important principle that informed and inspired the medieval mentality was the principle of order, and nowhere in medieval literature does that principle receive greater articulation than in the *Divine Comedy*. The signs of Dante's poetic universe all point to an underlying order, based principally on three concepts: hierarchy, analogy, and justice. Hierarchy is the proper sequential order of things along a vertical axis, in terms of the natural and inalienable right of privilege, authority, and precedence. Analogy identifies the inherent properties of resemblance and correspondence between otherwise dissimilar and unrelated things. Justice, both human and divine, is the proper degree of a being's desire (love) for another being with respect to that being's actions. These three concepts of order, exemplified by the three persons of the Trinity (God as supreme authority at the top of the chain of being, Christ as analogue linking the human with the divine, and the Holy Ghost as the spirit of just love uniting all things), find expression repeatedly and in sundry ways, both obvious and less obvious, throughout the poem: in the cosmology of the otherworld, in the suggested correspondences between different historical events, persons, moments, and phenomena, and in the ethically apposite congruity between a soul's life on earth and its fate after death.

Each of these basic principles is revealed by a wealth of images in the poem, images that speak for themselves and provide us with the conceptual signs of universal truth. This congruity between image and truth is possible by and large because Dante, with the rest of the Middle Ages, believed that the visible order of reality was perfectly coincident with the invisible one—less real and more defective, perhaps, but nevertheless perfectly coincident. Consequently, in constructing his poetic vision Dante relies in large measure on those rhetorical devices that stress the power of analogy: metaphor, allegory, symbol, simile, figure, and trope. In other words, Dante's concern with ontology has its analogue in his method of composition.

The image of Satan is a useful example of Dante's manner of illustrating the principles of hierarchy, analogy, and justice. Enshrined in a tomb at the precise center of the earth, at the lowest point in hell and the furthest in the universe from God, Satan, the great symbol of evil, sits locked in ice. On the hierarchical ladder of moral being, he is the basest of all living creatures, for between him and God lie all of humanity and the angels. Erect but immobile, he is a parody of the Unmoved Mover. With three pairs of batlike wings to the front and either side of his body flapping like banners, he appears to the pilgrim approaching from a distance like the cross on which Christ was crucified. The visual association is reinforced by Vergil's introit "Vexilla regis prodeunt inferni," a parody of a processional hymn, sung at vespers on Holy Friday, whose second verse is "Fulget crucis mysterium" ("shines forth the mystery of the cross"). The point is not that we are led to expect Christ and get Satan instead but that the diametric opposition between Christ and Satan, between good and evil of the same magnitude, can be established only by an outward appearance of likeness. Christ and Satan are proportionally though inversely related, but the analogy that links them is only provisional: the image stresses symmetry, not similarity. The monstrosity of Satan's three-faced visage, representing a deep-seated pride that multiplies the self in order better to experience its own being, likewise reflects the Divinity through its symmetry, here with the Trinity.

Dante the pilgrim and the reader with him discover the truth of Satan's inherent nature gradually, moment by moment, and nowhere does the poet explain the meaning of that image. Neither is our understanding of that image of evil fully complete at this juncture in the journey to God. We must wait until we come to the corresponding stages of symbolic resolution in the development of both the *Purgatorio* and the *Paradiso*. If Satan, the vortex that draws all evil downward into itself, is the climax of the *Inferno,* there are parallel and related moments in the other two *canticles* that fill out our understanding of his nature. In the *Purgatorio* it is the advent of Beatrice, whom Dante sees in the allegorical procession of the books of the Old and New Testaments, whose configuration delineates the shape of the cross. Beatrice stands on a chariot that follows directly behind the four Gospels and comes as *figura Christi*, at the precise moment when Christ appeared in history. The record of human sacred history is translated into a spatial image, and Beatrice occupies the moment and place of Christ's incarnation. This triumphal masque, laden with a sense of human history through which redemption from original and personal sin has been achieved, celebrates both a spirit of community wholly absent in the solitary, stationary, and self-sufficient figure of Satan, and an act of communion in the spiritual marriage of Dante to Beatrice.

This idea of community is deepened at the parallel climactic point in the narrative of the *Paradiso*, in the image of the white rose that collects in its petals, hierarchically, all of the saved souls beneath the direct luminescence of the Godhead. Here society transcends the transient concourse of history on the one hand and the personal and intimate union of two individuals on the other. In this celestial wedding of all souls, eternity subsumes time and the particular is replaced by the universal. The white rose, reaching upward toward the divine light, overcomes the downward pull of Satan's gravity while its rotundity converts the linear trajectory of the purgatorial procession into the endless circle of eternity.

The symmetrical placement of these three major images at the climax of each canticle, as a summation of the experience of each realm and an emblem of its entire significance, suggests that each must be read in the context of the others if we are to secure its full meaning. The *Divine Comedy* is a poem that for the most part unfolds its meaning gradually through a succession of related images, but it is one that possesses a synchronic as well as diachronic continuity. History, in Dante's vision, unfolds its order in a similar way not only through unbroken linear continuity but also through typological correspondences of figure and fulfillment between the events of the Old and New Testaments. And Dante's catalog of dead souls discloses the same principle of relatedness between the old and the new. Underscoring the moral dimension of that relation, he calls it "contrapasso": life on earth is a prefiguration of eternal fate, life beyond the grave the just fulfillment of earthly promise.

There are many ways to approach the teaching of the *Divine Comedy*, only one of which is through its imagery. I have chosen to stress Dante's imagery, in particular its unfolding nature, because it is a salient feature of his poetic style and one of the first things that arrests the reader's attention and compels complicity in the experience of the pilgrim's extraordinary journey. Dante's poetry, as many have observed, possesses an intensely communicative power to convey ideas through precise visual images, to translate abstract concepts like hierarchy, analogy, and justice into meaningful and convincing poetic realities.

I do not want to leave the reader with the feeling that the unfolding of the poem relies solely on a concatenation of symbolic images. There is another, complementary dimension to abstract reality in the poem, and that is psychological human realism. I am not thinking here of those remarkable instances in which Dante distills emotional experience into concrete images, as in many of his similes. I have in mind, rather, Dante's subtle delineation of an interior psychological state in his characters, revealed in the space of a few words, in a brief monologue or dialogue. Again it is not Dante's habit to explain his meanings. We learn to intuit those meanings by relating one moment of experience to other, analogous moments. The *Divine Comedy* is full of such internal echoes, resonances, and reflections of itself. Vergil's severe chastisement of Dante's delay in the journey (*Purgatorio* V), when the pilgrim turns to study in perhaps too prolonged a manner the amazement of the lethargic penitents, might be explained in part as Vergil's overreaction to Cato's censure moments earlier (at the end of Canto II) for a similar delay. Dante does not explain Vergil's extreme reaction, but in the immediate context of Cato's reproach we can discern the motivation for that behavior.

Not all things in the *Divine Comedy* are equally accessible to critical investigation; nor are they meant to be. Whatever veiled references we can discover in the cryptograms of the Veltro, the DXV, or the three beasts, a part of their final meaning surely consists of the sense of mystery, enigma, and impenetrability that they instill in the reader. But Dante has it both ways, as it were, for there is no better way to induce the reader into the act of looking for meaning than to place it just beyond immediate grasp. Mystery and obscurity stir the imagination and compel an active search for meaning. If my examples have succeeded in demonstrating anything, I hope it is to emphasize that the production of meaning in the *Divine Comedy* consists of a gradual process of revelation, a process that dramatizes the manner by which knowledge is acquired. The teacher therefore has a double duty of helping students to understand not only the poem's meanings but how those meanings are made manifest.

ON TEACHING THE *INFERNO*

Wallace Fowlie

Each time the Dante semester returns in my teaching schedule—
Monday, Wednesday, Friday for fifteen weeks—with all those class
hours to be given to the thirty-four cantos of the first canticle, I plot
and replot the purpose of the course, trying to decide what to emphasize and how to emphasize it. Every two or three years these prep-
arations vary because of the historical moment in literary criticism, in
religious awareness, in the preoccupations of students. The spring of
1970, when I first taught Dante at Duke University, was different in all
those respects from the spring of 1979, when I taught the *Inferno* for
the first time as an emeritus professor.

Some of the semesters I plan to accentuate the psychic rather than
the moral and the religious. I plan to consider Dante's descent into hell
as a descent into his subconscious and his past in order to understand
why he is lost, why he is estranged. I argue with myself and my students that to justify and understand oneself, one has to know the worst
about oneself. By the "worst" I mean those experiences, often forgot-
ten or concealed, that have alienated one from the order of the world.

The guiding thought of the course would therefore be this: Dante
must descend into hell. Vergil tells him in Canto I that there is no other
choice. The word *cammino*, the "way," appears in the first line of the

67

Inferno and in the seventh from the last line. This "way" leads to knowledge of the worst, that which must be known before we can reach the best. And Dante's hell certainly presents the worst: Dante avoids nothing that is bad, corrupt, or malicious. Hell is the world reinvented. It is the world written in Italian verse. It is composed of one fantasy picture after another, and each one is a form of obsession that, if allowed to remain in the form of an obsession, would cause serious suffering in a human being, would impede him or her from self-realization and ultimate salvation, even salvation in the purely human sense.

I always felt more secure in teaching my courses in French literature—Proust or the symbolist poets, for example—but Dante exalts and excites me more. I have to plan each lesson on each canto more carefully and choose the words I want to emphasize, the lines I want to make as memorable as possible, the characters and scenes I want students to remember for life. As I prepare the lessons, I often think back to the course I took at Harvard with Charles Grandgent when we read the *Divine Comedy* in his edition: the Italian text with the voluminous notes on each page and the brief outline-introduction to each canto.

It was the last time he gave his famous course, and we were awed by his scholarly edition of the poem and by his age and his quiet manner. We were, I must confess, disappointed that all he did in class, throughout the entire year, was to have us translate the Italian text as it appeared in his edition. From time to time he read aloud a passage in Italian and then asked one of us to translate it. But the hour was largely filled by our own awkward, hesitating translations. Grandgent offered no commentary on the text, as if all he had to say had been consigned to the footnotes of his book. If once every two or three weeks one of us dared ask a question, he would answer in a most complete and satisfactory way. Thus we realized he had not put everything he knew into his edition.

The eminent Harvard teachers and translators (Longfellow, Charles Eliot Norton, George Santayana, Charles H. Grandgent) have been succeeded in this generation by a few brilliant American Dante scholars: Charles S. Singleton, Thomas G. Bergin, Francis Fergusson, John Freccero, Mark Musa. Singleton, surely the best Dante scholar in the world today, has now revised and reissued Grandgent's edition of the *Divine Comedy*. Many teachers today use a bilingual edition, and many of them, like myself, prepare a lecture-discussion class. That was not Grandgent's method! He listened to our translation in class and corrected us gently. No paper to write, no quiz to take, only a final exam, largely made up of long passages to translate! I doubt if any class in an American university today would tolerate such an absence of pedagogy and stimulation. We learned some Italian from Grandgent, but we had to learn by ourselves, outside the class, elements of what today we would call a critical-interpretive approach to Dante.

Each time I resume the teaching of the *Inferno*, it is with the same self-acknowledged confession: Dante is the fountainhead of literature for me, the source. I have never felt the need of going before him to a detailed study of earlier writers: to the chansons de geste or Chrétien, to the Greek or Latin poets. They are all there in Dante, in places where I can see them, not analyzed, but used and illuminated, assigned to some niche in a vast reproduction of the world and the apocalyptic life of the world beyond the world.

More than any other single work, the *Inferno* has given me the fullest realization of what literature is. Dante is the supreme example of the artist who seizes everything around him and uses everything within him: mind, heart, sexuality. Everything is to be used and conquered. And because he is satisfied with nothing less than everything, his work abounds with enigmas and inconsistencies. They are countless, there in the texts, even in the early work, the *Vita nuova*, and he wanted them as enigmas and left them as such.

Nothing exists by itself in the poem, no figure, no landscape, no metaphor, no sin. Not even the poet himself. Everything is illuminated by everything else. His art is a close network of relations: secret, invisible, and visible relations between things, between things and people, between their aspirations and their faults, between God and his creatures. Because of this complexity, the *Divine Comedy* demands of its readers a full concentration and a willingness to subordinate to it, temporarily, the rest of life. Before it gives itself to the reader, the *Inferno* has to be examined over and over again. Then, one day, like a piece of music that has been listened to many times, it is there intact in the life of the reader, as part of his or her knowledge and being. This phenomenon of knowledge comes about not through research in the modern sense but through the penetration of a world, through the seeing of a world that exists in words, images, and characters created by words.

More than a device in teaching, the relating of Dante to contemporary literature is an obligation. The modern world has no purely poetic work comparable to the *Divine Comedy*, but there are works of prose that have the linguistic tenseness of poetry and that reveal in their power of imagery what poetry is able to reveal: the works of Proust and Joyce. In fact, the word *inferno* would not be a misnomer in designating *Remembrance of Things Past* or *Ulysses*. Each is a world in itself organized into scenes of tests and punishments. Each of the three works offers as a protagonist a writer (Dante, Marcel, and Stephen) who narrates his voyage through the episodes and who also participates to some degree in the episodes. All three protagonist-writers are voyeurs as well as actors. In each story, their principal adventure is preceded by a form of prelude, a mysterious early work in which the writer tests himself and announces the greater work to come. It is the *Vita nuova* for Dante, a secretive and almost esoteric introduction to the *Divine Comedy*. For Proust, it is *Swann's Way*, a prefiguration of Marcel's love for Gilberte and Albertine, and of his desire to know the two worlds, the two "ways" of Swann and Guermantes. Then, finally, for Joyce, the story of Stephen Dedalus is first told in *Portrait of the Artist as a Young Man* before being continued in *Ulysses*.

Dante was not obsessed by time as Proust was. His power of a poet is that of seizing time and inventing for it a pulsation that beats in the present. But Proust is time's victim. The descent in *Remembrance of Things Past* is not one into hell—he is already there—but a universal descent into the void. Because of life's fluidity and ephemeral aspect, death is real for Proust. The metamorphosis that death will bring is simply a mask for the degradation of life. Dante, who has no dread of time, no obsession with it, would call it that force that assassinates and at the same time sustains life and promotes it.

Like every other major artist, Dante was concerned with leaving a work that would never betray him. The face of such a work is always partially in a shadow. This lesson is the inevitable result of every reading and discussion on a canto. The luminous and shadowy parts of any such complex work as Dante's poem come from the world's celebration of it. Literary fame comes on and goes off like the flashing light of a beacon, like the inevitable sequence of day and night, comprehension and misunderstanding. It takes time for a work of this magnitude to rediscover its order and to reinvent its reality. The wisdom of Dante and Shakespeare, of Proust and Joyce, is so covered with scars, with all the imperfections of words, whether they be Italian or English or French, that we often read them and believe we see what we do not actually see.

Is the world outside of time a stumbling block for students today? The finite story of humankind, in our lives and in the history of our times, is carried over by Dante into the eternal world, and yet the finite form of our first life never disappears. A transformation has taken place, but through the transformation, one can see the finiteness of the earlier life. The miracle of Dante's creation is this power of giving to each scene a realistic contour and precision, and at the same time, of giving to readers the impression that they are watching a scene belonging to another world, the world beyond death, or at least the fantasy world of obsessions and nightmares.

From the fourteenth to the twentieth century: how, if at all, has our history changed? In a general sense, it is not difficult to make the transition from the dead in the underworld regions of Homer and Vergil, and the damned souls in Dante's *Inferno* to the descent into the subterranean cosmos of the personality that persons today can achieve, especially at moments of great crisis in their lives, when they need to consult the dead of their race, who still live in them, and the dead figures of their own personalities, who desire to return to the living self and resume an interrupted existence.

The subconscious is endless in a human being and as deep as Dante makes his hell. It is filled with as many grimacing, sad, and violent figures as those we encounter in the Italian poem. The speech of the lost figures in our own life is as enigmatic, as dramatic, as elliptical, as the speech of Filippo Argenti, Farinata, and Cavalcante, father of Guido Cavalcanti. In the circles of his hell Dante encounters ghosts of the past who have some relation with his own moral scruples and defects, as today we encounter in medical consultations and self-analyses the origins of our conflicts.

Dante's spirits and the realms they inhabit are graphically portrayed. Only the size of these realms is incommensurable with the earth and difficult for the reader to grasp. It is the difference between earth and eternity, and yet Dante keeps reminding his readers that it is on earth where our eternal existence is determined. Everything on earth is eternalized in the realms beyond the earth. Likewise, trials and defects and devastations from the very distant and very immediate past are prolonged and eternalized through us. The funnel of Dante's hell in its ever-deepening function constitutes the landscape of sins, which today in our more tentative and more evasive language we call obsessions.

CRITICAL APPROACHES TO TEACHING THE *DIVINE COMEDY*

READING THE *DIVINE COMEDY:* A TEXTUAL APPROACH

Christopher Kleinhenz

The approaches to teaching the *Divine Comedy* are many and diverse, and none is satisfactory and complete in itself. To be understood and properly appreciated, Dante's poem, like all other truly great works of literature, must be read carefully and examined from a number of perspectives. But reading the *Divine Comedy* is not a simple process; indeed, it requires time, patience, and perseverance. Just as the art connoisseur must learn to "see" and the music critic to "hear," so the attentive student of Dante must learn to "read," to understand the text of the *Divine Comedy*, to become thoroughly familiar with its language, rhythms, stylistic devices, images, and patterns of speech. In my year course on the *Divine Comedy* I have gradually evolved and refined my pedagogical methods over the past decade to achieve the following goals: that the students understand the *Divine Comedy* both in its general overall dimensions and in its particulars, that they appreciate the poem as the crowning literary and intellectual achievement of the Middle Ages, and that they recognize its timeless qualities and message, which remains a vital force in the twentieth century. I hope, moreover, that they learn to approach the work from a variety of perspectives and, thus, remain flexible in their interpretation, allowing the poem to open itself up to them.

Because I am most interested in having my students learn to understand and appreciate the poetry of the *Divine Comedy*, my methodology begins with, and relies heavily on, the language of the text itself, on the linguistic, rhetorical, and stylistic constructs, and on the aesthetics and dynamics of the poetry. A close reading and analysis of the text is, in my opinion, the single most important part of a Dante course and the necessary prelude to all further discussion. This familiarity with the text is the first stage of what I would term a coming to grips with the art and craft of Dante the poet. From this awareness of textual minutiae and their importance in a number of interrelated areas, we proceed to a consideration of larger topics (the creation of scenes, landscapes, characters), greater domains (the organization and unity of entire episodes, cantos, circles, regions), and finally all-embracing issues of paramount importance (the *Divine Comedy* as a unified work of art).

While I adapt my methodology to the different situations and problems of the *Divine Comedy* (for example, an allegorical/typological/ archetypal approach in *Inf.* I–II; a linguistic/psychological/stylistic one in *Inf.* XIII), the text remains the common ground and the necessary basis and starting point for all discussion. We do not translate in class. We do not merely retell the story of the pilgrim's journey. I assume a basic understanding of the literal meaning of Dante's text; and therefore our extended discussions in class are devoted to *how* and *why* he says what he says, to considerations of aesthetic structure, to questions of style, allegory and typology, to matters of a philosophical and theological nature, to analogues with the earlier and later literary tradition, and to the relation of the *Divine Comedy* to contemporary developments in medieval art, historiography, science, and so on.

The class is composed primarily of Italian majors at the graduate and advanced undergraduate levels and usually several other students from related fields (French, English, comparative literature, etc.). This sort of distribution has been extremely helpful and stimulating. Although class time is usually devoted to discussion, I begin the term with several lectures on the general historical and cultural milieu of the late thirteenth century and on the more specific topics of Dante's life and minor works. Students are encouraged to become familiar with certain historically oriented works and other background materials, specifically with the *Vita nuova, De Monarchia,* and selections from *De Vulgari Eloquentia, Rime, Convivio,* and the *Epistles.* We spend the remainder of the academic year reading the cantos of the entire *Divine Comedy* in sequence, preparing and discussing one or two cantos for each meeting. The students are provided with study questions to guide their reading, and in this way the discussion has a form and is somewhat controlled. In the classroom, then, we work together as a team to find answers to these questions. Because of their diverse preparation and interests, however, the students through their comments often open up many new areas for investigation. We explore these new directions as far as our capacities and pertinence to the text will allow.

Certain questions and problems inevitably arise in a reading of the *Divine Comedy* for which there is no single, specific interpretation in the text (for example, the significance of the "lupa," "leone," and "lonza" in *Inf.* I, or the identity of "colui / che fece per viltade il gran rifiuto" in *Inf.* III, or the meaning of the "corda" in *Inf.* XVI). Although I encourage my students to become familiar with the vast critical literature on Dante and to use the standard commentaries and reference works, I discourage their attempting to resolve every crux in the poem immediately and often solely on the authority of secondary sources. For problems of this sort I generally ask them to withhold judgment, to wait until they have read more of the poem—that is, until such a time that the poem itself has yielded up more clues to shed light on the possible meaning of the episode. Since Dante has carefully and consciously woven his verbal fabric, the many lexical associations, echoes, and correspondences are present by choice not chance, and thus close attention to the text is indeed the best way of discovering Dante's poetic strategies.

The textual approach serves to highlight and render even more prominent these occasions of verbal and/or semantic similarity. One such fascinating feature of the *Divine Comedy* is its capacity to gloss itself (for example, Casella's song and Cato's reprimand in *Purg.* II as a gloss on *Inf.* V; the valley of the princes in *Purg.* VII–VIII as a reflection of Limbo). Another is the high and significant degree of "intertextuality" one encounters in the poem (for example, Vergil's exhortation to the pilgrim in *Inf.* II and that of Mercury to Aeneas in *Aeneid* IV, the presence in *Purg.* XXX of one Vergilian verse ["Manibus . . . date lilia plenis," *Aeneid* VI. 883] and other echoes from the *Aeneid* and the *Georgics*, the paraphrase and adaptation of the Paternoster in *Purg.* XI, direct citations from Latin hymns [*Inf.* XXXIV; *Purg.* VIII, etc.] and the Vulgate [*Purg.* XVII, XXVII, etc.]). These passages are not, of course, simple verbal borrowings but assume new resonances and significance in their new context. By channeling our attention along these two separate but similar lines of inquiry, we are able to see ever more clearly how Dante came to create certain scenes and episodes, and, even more importantly, we may begin to perceive the order of the external medieval world and its ultimate informing power on the *Di-*

vine Comedy. These approaches to the poem are essentially later developments, extensions as it were of my basic textual methodology brought to its logical conclusion.

The actual mechanics of the textual approach can be illustrated by considering the importance to literary analysis of four principal phenomena: (1) key words; (2) semantic shifts; (3) variant readings; and (4) *hapax legomena*. Their presentation here is intended only to demonstrate some of the possibilities of the textual method and does not presume to cover the area completely. One of the many ways in which Dante organizes his cantos is the use and repetition of key words, an understanding of which helps to clarify and focus attention on the larger meaning. A case in point is *Inferno* IV, where *onore* (and its derivatives *orrevol*, *onorare*, etc.) occurs eight times. Obviously, then, "honor" is crucial to Dante's overall conception of the "nobile castello." We know the reasons are several. In addition to reinforcing the Aristotelian dictum expressed in *De Monarchia* that "Honor is the reward of virtue" ("Cum honor sit premium virtutis," II. iii. 6–7; cf. *Nicomachean Ethics* IV. 3. 1123 b 35), Dante is here laying the groundwork for his eventual acceptance by the other poets as "sesto tra cotanto senno," a short-lived triumph that is undercut by the pilgrim's failure to contend with lust and his resulting swoon in the following canto. The high esteem in which Dante the pilgrim holds these virtuous souls in Limbo is symptomatic of his general misappraisal of earthly goodness vis-à-vis the operation of Divine Justice. For example, in *Inferno* VI he asks Ciacco about several illustrious Florentines for whose earthly deeds he has great respect:

> Farinata e 'l Tegghiaio, che fuor sì degni,
> Iacopo Rusticucci, Arrigo e 'l Mosca
> e li altri ch' a ben far puoser li 'ngegni.
> (*Inf.* VI. 79–81)

Ciacco reveals that they are punished in lower hell, and thus the pilgrim comes to realize that worldly honor is not in itself sufficient for salvation. So, remembering Dante's insistence on *onore* and the general situation in *Inferno* IV, we then note its appearance and meaning in other contexts. In our reading of the entire *Divine Comedy* we find thirty-seven occurrences of *onore* and its derivatives, and in each one the term refers to worldly fame and its ephemeral quality. We may then look in retrospect to the initial emphasis given *onore* in *Inferno* IV and recognize that through the use of this word Dante is able to present the value of earthly honor in a dubious, if not negative, light. The trembling air, the darkness that surrounds the self-illuminated noble castle and separates it from the true light and true source of goodness, and the sighs of those virtuous souls therein imprisoned are all eloquent testimonies to the manner in which Dante the poet views earthly honor: sufficient as a temporal reward but insufficient for salvation.

A close reading of the text can reveal how certain words undergo a semantic shift in the passage from hell to purgatory and paradise. We may observe one example of this phenomenon in *Inferno* VI, where Vergil silences three-headed Cerberus:

> E 'l duca mio distese le sue spanne,
> prese la terra, e con piene le pugna
> la gittò dentro a le bramose canne.
> Qual è quel cane ch'abbaiando agogna,
> e si racqueta poi che 'l pasto morde,
> ché solo a divorarlo intende e pugna,
> cotai si fecer quelle facce lorde
> de lo demonio Cerbero, che 'ntrona
> l'anime sì, ch'esser vorrebber sorde.
> (*Inf.* VI. 25–33)

Our attention is called to the word *pugna* because of its repetition in equivocal rhyme. An investigation of the use of *pugno* and its derivatives reveals that there is a changeover in its meaning, from negative to positive connotations, in the passage from hell to paradise. The presence of *pugna* in *Inferno* VI takes on greater significance in light of its later uses in the *Inferno* to indicate greedy possession ("questi resurgeranno del sepulcro / col pugno chiuso" [VII. 57–58]), the rebellion of the giants against the Olympian gods ("la pugna di Flegra" [XIV. 58]), and hateful combat ("col pugno li percosse l'epa croia" [XXX. 102]). In the *Purgatorio*, however, the term characterizes the gentle conflict between dew and sun ("quando noi fummo là 've la rugiada / pugna col sole" [I. 121–22]) and signals the "victory" of Pope Adrian V's will over that of the pilgrim ("Contra miglior voler voler mal pugna" [XX. 1]). Finally, in the *Paradiso* it indicates the struggle and victory of the just and virtuous over the forces of evil: the fight for the Empire ("Tu sai ch'el [the eagle] fece in Alba sua dimora / per trecento anni e oltre, infino al fine / che i tre a' tre pugnar per lui ancora" [VI. 37–39]) and the disciples' fervent struggle to spread the gospel ("e quel tanto sonò ne le sue guance, / sì ch'a pugnar per accender la fede / de l'Evangelio fero scudo e lance" [XXIX. 112–14]).

Variant readings in the text are also rich sources of commentary. One well-known variant occurs in *Inferno* III: "E io ch'avea d'error [d'orror] la testa cinta" (31). On the one hand, if the pilgrim's head were "cinta d'error," this would prompt him to ask the question in the following verses: "Maestro, che è quel ch'i' odo? / e che gent' è che par nel duol sì vinta?" (32–33). On the other hand, the head "cinta d'error" is certainly a striking image, one that is a logical product of the terrifying atmosphere of the vestibule, and one that has, moreover, Vergilian resonances (*Aeneid* II. 559; IV. 280; VI. 559). Another example is the variant reading in *Inferno* XIV, where Capaneus is referred to as

> quel grande che non par che curi
> lo 'ncendio e giace dispettoso e torto,
> sì che la pioggia non par che 'l maturi [marturi].
> (*Inf.* XIV. 46–48)

Marturi in the sense of "torments, tortures" is eminently logical. *Maturi* ("ripens"), however, would appear to be a better poetic choice because of its associations with the general conception and characterization of pride (*superbia*) as an unripe (*acerbo*) state (see the description of Vanni Fucci [*Inf.* XXV. 18] and Lucifer [*Par.* XIX. 46–48]). Evaluation of variant readings allows the student the opportunity to look into the creative process and to attempt to determine the various possibilities within the contingencies and necessities of the text.

Another advantage of close textual analysis is that by recognizing and elucidating *hapax legomenon*, the single occurrence of a word, we are able to discover its particular textual function. For example, in *Inferno* XXXI Nimrod and the giants in general are associated both verbally and visually with other proud sinners: Farinata, Capaneus, Lucifer. We know from *De Vulgari Eloquentia* that Dante viewed the disobedience of the first parents as the first example of pride, and, as such, it is the technical counterpart of Lucifer's rebellion and the assault of the giants on Olympus. The similarity between Adam and Eve and the giants is enhanced by the unique use of the term *perizoma* to describe the covering afforded Nimrod by the side of the pit ("la ripa, ch'era perizoma / dal mezzo in giù" [61f]). In the story of the Fall in Genesis, the word *perizomata* refers to the aprons Adam and Eve fashion to hide their newly discovered nakedness, thus revealing to the Lord their disobedience of his command ("Et aperti sunt oculi amborum: cumque cognovissent se esse nudos, consuerunt folia ficus, et fecerunt sibi perizomata" [III. 7]). In the same way as this transgression resulted in banishment from the Garden of Eden, a punishment laden with both individual significance and universal consequences, the effect of Nimrod's insubordination in building the Tower of Babel was the confusion of his own speech and that of the world's languages. The pride of the creature, transformed into rebellion against his Creator, has resulted, respectively, in the loss of innocence and purity and in the loss of a single and divine language. By paying special attention to *hapax legomenon,* we are able to open up certain passages for extensive commentary and to reveal thereby much of the richness and allusive capacity of the text.

In this brief essay I have attempted to convey some of the basic notions and general principles of my textual approach to the *Divine Comedy.* Such an approach is not new, nor is it uniquely mine. But just as one cannot teach the poem in a vacuum, without reference to anything "outside" it, so one cannot be a teacher of Dante without using a number of approaches simultaneously. Indeed, my own work as a teacher of Dante has been influenced and determined by the example of a number of fine scholars, to whom I owe an immense debt of gratitude.

One final observation in conclusion. In approaching the *Divine Comedy* I believe we should be wary of being overawed initially by the epithet *divine,* that is, by its larger historical, cultural, philosophical, and theological dimensions, by the nimbus of glory that surrounds the text. Its divinity is best approached and finally discerned by beginning concretely with the poet's and writer's *Commedia,* that is, with the verbal constructs, words, images, figures, stylistic and rhetorical devices that Dante put together and that in their interrelation and totality become the poem to which his later readers accorded the attribute "divine."

THE *DIVINE COMEDY:* TEXT AND CONTEXTS

Rachel Jacoff

My teaching of Dante has been deeply influenced by the teachers who made the poem come alive for me, in particular Joseph A. Mazzeo, who first encouraged my interest in Dante, and John Freccero, whose Dante course remains a model of teaching as the highest form of thinking aloud. There are many ways of teaching a poem as rich and complex as the *Divine Comedy*, and part of the pleasure of such an enterprise is that one goes on continually rethinking both one's critical and one's pedagogical relation to it. I have taught the *Divine Comedy* in one-semester courses as well as in courses devoted to larger subjects, such as medieval literature in translation and a medieval studies seminar on typology, but since I believe that it is a central text in any serious literature curriculum, I prefer to teach it as a full-year course. Even if the poem is read in translation, a full year is necessary to give students the background material and prolonged attention to detail that enable them to feel they are on intimate terms with the poem rather than intimidated by it.

Although I prefer to teach Dante in translation so as to reach as many students as possible, I feel that such a course is also an important way to generate interest in Italian. A teacher who knows Dante in Italian can take advantage of a bilingual text to reveal particular aspects of the original in ways that encourage students to go on to the study of Italian. A bilingual text serves as a constant reminder that we are reading a translation, but it also makes possible continuous allusion to the original and the discussion of specifically linguistic matters: nuances of rhythm, neologisms, unusual rhyme schemes and their particular effects, and the problems of translating certain words or passages. This is hardly the equivalent of reading the *Divine Comedy* in its own incomparably dense, various, and richly suggestive musicality, but it can point students in that direction.

In my full-year course we begin at once with the first canto of the *Inferno*. I go slowly in the first weeks in order to provide time for background material and to explain fundamental interpretive principles. While we are reading the opening cantos, the students are also reading the *Aeneid* and preparing a paper on Book VI for the second week of class. I try to focus discussion in the early classes on the relation of these two texts as a way of engaging students in the terms of Dante's dramatization of Vergil and Vergil's text and also as a way of suggesting at the start that Dante's use of other texts is dialectical, at once complementary and corrective. After the students have written on the *Aeneid,* we go on to a more generalized discussion of Dante's use of biblical typology in connection with Canto IV. We have spoken of the Exodus typology from the beginning of the course, but here we get into the figure of the harrowing of hell, its application to Dante's own journey and his "harrowing," up to a point, of the great figures of classical antiquity. This unorthodox and poignant canto helps us to see that typology is a matter of not simply equivalences, but differences as well.

In the opening weeks of the course I try to introduce background material and thematic issues gradually and always in relation to specific episodes in the poem. Certain cantos call for historical and political information, others for literary, philosophical, biblical, or theological glossing. The most important thing is for students to get into the poem, to learn the kinds of questions they should be asking about it, and to discover their need for knowledge in reading it, a need that should make their relation to footnotes and other outside information more lively. But this information must be balanced against a sense of the immediate power of the text, its human and dramatic appeal. It is important to make the poem illuminate itself as much as possible, to keep alluding to passages already discussed in order to define new situations either by contrast or by comparison. Inevitably, readings of specific parts of the poem begin to form part of a coherent reading of the whole. Instead of seeing the *Inferno* as a series of great figures or highlights, the students develop a sense of the relation of the structure of the poem to its narrative power; the recurrent question of how to react to the various seductions of the strong personalities of the *Inferno* becomes more complex and contextually specific.

In the first semester we read the *Aeneid* and the *Inferno*, followed by the *Vita nuova* and two of the *rime petrose*. I have found that it is easier for students to attend to the intensity of the *Vita nuova* after they have learned how to read the *Divine Comedy*. It also seems a useful strategy to end the first semester with the kind of anticipation toward Beatrice that the *Vita nuova* generates and that is so fundamental to the *Purgatorio*. Lately I have taught some of the *rime petrose* as well in order to suggest the range of Dante's stylistic and imaginative power.

In the spring semester we read the *Purgatorio* and the *Paradiso*. In the *Purgatorio* I am particularly interested in the dramatization of literary influence (Cantos XX–XXVI), the typological structure of the terraces, and the special tonality of human tenderness that is characteristic of this canticle. For me, the *Purgatorio* is the scene of the most moving human encounters, those of Vergil and Statius and of Dante and Beatrice. Memory and desire come together most tellingly in this canticle; its images of friendship and its exploration of the possibilities of the human imagination are deeply resonant.

It is in teaching the *Paradiso*, however, that I feel most challenged. The fascination of this canticle does not derive from its human interest, although actually it is filled with interesting human narratives. The emphasis seems rather to be on the beauty of the patterns created in and by the poetry; sometimes I think of the *Paradiso* as the ultimate *ballet blanc*. It is marvelous to see how Dante literally makes matter into spirit, metaphorizing the cosmos, for example, taking astronomical details and giving them moral significance. Another pleasure for students of the *Paradiso* is the retrospective gloss it provides on the earlier canticles. Here, in a sense, is the model; the rest is copy, whether as infernal parody or purgatorial anticipation. The *Paradiso* is, as Dante's addresses to the reader make explicit, an absolutely daring adventure, and it should be presented in such terms. John Freccero's work on the *Paradiso*, especially his dense article on Canto X, has pointed the way for a reading of the canticle that insists on seeing its poetics as a manifestation of its theology and at the same time honoring its immense sophistication about the limits of its own referentiality.[1] Although Charles Grandgent begins his commentary on the *Paradiso* by calling it the "most medieval part of the poem," and although it is a cliché that the idea of unchanging happiness does not attract us any longer, in fact the *Paradiso* is the most poetically self-reflexive part of the poem, the place where the most serious and interesting questions about poetry itself are implied. It is extraordinary, too, in imagining a world beyond guilt and in giving us vicarious access to experience otherwise unimaginable.

One calls on many exegetical procedures in explicating the *Divine Comedy;* at different points in the poem some approaches seem more useful than others. In recent years I have found that my own strongest interest is in Dante's way of using previous texts, both his own and others', particularly the *Aeneid* and the Bible. I have come to connect my interest in intertextuality with principles of typological allegory I have learned from the work of Erich Auerbach, Charles Singleton, A. C. Charity, John Freccero, Giuseppe Mazzotta, and Robert Hollander. I think of typology in its largest sense as a paradigm for the fullest possible reading experience. In the common historical view, typology developed as a way of reading, specifically as a way of reading the Old Testament from the vantage point of the New. As John Hollander has suggested, thinking of the Old Testament by that name rather than as the Hebrew Bible suggests that a text once regarded as complete in itself is now regarded as significant primarily in relation to a subsequent text.[2]

Typology takes various forms in patristic and medieval exegetical practice and theory, but we might say that it is a way of positing a fourfold temporality for any given event significant in salvation history. Such an event possesses an Old Testament prefigurative historical reality, a New Testament fulfillment in the life of Christ (or by extension the life of the Church or the sacraments), a present-time analogue in the soul of any Christian who reenacts the biblical event in his or her own life (what A. C. Charity calls, in *Events and Their Afterlife,* "applied typology," the *pro nobis* dimension of any salvation event) and an anticipated and ultimate version in the world to come at the end of time. This formulation, of course, brings to mind Dante's own mode of glossing the Psalm of Exodus in the letter to Can Grande, the dedicatory letter to the *Paradiso* whose authority and importance have been made clear in several recent studies. Complications arise in any consistent attempt to apply this mode of unfolding meaning to Dante's poem, and, as far as I can see, it does not provide a total approach to all the questions raised by the poem. Yet it has a great advantage over other more "spatial" notions of allegory that tended to posit equivalences (Vergil is Reason, for example), and it allows us to recognize that a given figure in the poem may have more than one figural role, as Beatrice does, for example.

Apart from the question of typological readings of the *Divine Comedy*, the medieval typological schema offers a useful model for talking about relations between texts. If we take the *Divine Comedy* as the center of our attention, it plays a role analogous to that of the New Testament in the conventional schema. It sets out to fulfill and complete certain prior classical texts whose meaning it redefines in the process. At the same time the *Divine Comedy* also "applies" biblical typology insofar as Dante reenacts certain key actions of Christ's life or those of other biblical figures, both prophetic and apostolic. Not only Dante but other characters (or actions) in the poem participate in such typological readings. The *Divine Comedy* has yet a further *pro nobis* dimension in the life and mind of any of its readers who find a way to apply, assimilate, and relate imaginatively to it. For us as readers in our own historical moment this means finding the poem's psychological and phenomenological validity in terms that translate its theological truths into secular insights. The poem's literary futurity might be thought of as its anagoge. No one has set out to "fulfill" Dante as Dante did Vergil, yet the poem's fruitfulness as a source of literary inspiration is ongoing, and never more so than in our own century. I suppose as many people of my generation read Dante because of T. S. Eliot as read Vergil for the sake of Dante.

Such a fourfold temporality might be posited in the abstract for other important literary works, but it has explicit relevance to the *Divine Comedy* precisely because Dante consciously establishes a typological relation between his own text and its chosen predecessors (even in the *Vita nuova* he had hinted at this kind of relation between his poetry and Guido Cavalcanti's in his playful meditation on the Giovanna-Primavera etymologies in Chapter XXIV). With respect to the Bible and to salvation history, Dante's journey depends for its existence and in many of its details on the prior model, mediated, one must add, by exegetical tradition. The issue of intertextuality with respect to Dante's classical models, especially Vergil, is part of the larger problem of the relation between the pre-Christian and Christian cultures. The longer I teach the *Divine Comedy*, the more its most poignant energies seem to be involved in the tension between the poem's commitment to Christian truth and to classical wisdom or, to put it in Giorgio Padoan's terms, between its eschatological claims and its literary ambitions.[3] Dante dramatizes this tension most visibly in his presentation of Vergil, and he goes on doing so even after Vergil has disappeared as a character from the *Divine Comedy*. Classical literature is seen to have a semiprophetic relation to Christian truth, both anticipating and falling short of it. At times, as in the Earthly Paradise when Matelda tells Vergil that ancient literature "perhaps dreamed" the reality now present or in *Paradiso* IV when Beatrice gives an allegorical reading of Plato's *Timaeus* that redeems its truth value, the relation between ancient and Christian truth is consonant and is a source of smiles; at times, and fundamentally, the ultimate disparity between them is a source of tears, as it is in Vergil's disappearance, or of astonishment, as it is when we learn that Ripheus, a minor character in the *Aeneid*, is saved, while neither Vergil nor Aeneas is.

For Americans the most important work on Dante in the past few decades has led toward a unifying view of the *Divine Comedy*, an emphasis on its patterns, symmetries, and progressive unfolding of meaning. The nineteenth-century readings that saw the poem as undermined by Dante's covert sympathies with the "great" sinners, or believed that its structure and thought were separable from its poetry, or considered that its extraordinary realism unbalanced its religious premises have given way to others that respect the poem's integrity and its unity of aspiration and method. We are all heirs to this remarkable turnabout, and we are all in particular debt to Charles Singleton and Erich Auerbach for the change. Nonetheless, in our teaching it is important, I think, to keep alive the sense of the problematic in the poem, both for ourselves and for our students. It is crucial to see that the poem raises problems as well as solves them and that there are specific areas of human and intellectual tension that cannot be waved away by recourse to theological glosses. Interpretation is ongoing and subject to revision, and I like to share the fact that I have changed my reading of certain passages or that I have learned something new in a current rereading, or that a new book or article has changed a previous assumption. And students' responses also help us to understand where and how the poem remains difficult.

The notion of alterity has become important recently in discussions of medieval literature. I would say that the *Divine Comedy* is a poem that demands a double perspective from us: we must attempt to enter the poem's world without assuming either that we could do so perfectly or that we could remain within such a frame. We must honor its irrevocable otherness, but we need both knowledge and imagination to make that otherness intelligible; and we need the experience to make clear why the poem speaks to us of our own lives as well as of its own time. This double perspective allows us to be passionate about Dante without being either sentimental or in "bad faith." One works this out in one's own way, but the issue demands a kind of honesty not always apparent in writing about Dante.

Teaching the *Divine Comedy*, then, is largely a matter of two different procedures or movements. One must create the proper contexts (historical, biblical, philosophical, theological, and literary) to reveal the poem's depth and the resonance of its details. This is a matter of not simply adducing sources or influences but trying to see how Dante works with these sources, how he shapes, changes, and comments on the texts and traditions he inherited. To make this grammar of allusion as rich and intelligible as possible, it is useful to read aloud or summarize key passages or texts one wishes to discuss in relation to the poem. The role, for example, of Statius' *Thebaid* in Dante's poem is vital; although no one would ask undergraduates to read the *Thebaid*, students should understand its role in the *Divine Comedy* and should recognize the allusions to it as forming a pattern, a configuration that gives Dante's outburst (after Ugolino's speech) against Pisa as a "new Thebes" its true valence. In my experience, biblical allusions are often as obscure as classical allusions to our students, and there, too, we can create the larger context of a particular reference. In this way, the *Divine Comedy* becomes a kind of lens on a whole world of texts and concerns.

But one also wants to bring the poem into relation to our own world, both in experiential and in literary terms. It has the power to illuminate and to be illuminated by our own time. Modern literature is filled with allusions to Dante, and often these become a way of focusing some particular aspect of Dante's appeal or meaning. I try to speak about such things in relation to particular episodes or lines in the *Divine Comedy* that were important to other writers, sometimes for the "wrong" reasons or in ways that suggest an attempt to "correct" Dante, as Eliot does, for example, in the encounter in "Little Gidding," where the Brunettoesque figure delivers an attack on humanistic notions of language and literature.

Dante provides us in the *Divine Comedy* with many models for reading as an activity seen both *in malo* (Francesca) and *in bono* (Statius). He even provides us with a model for constructive misreading in the case of Statius. But the many models within the poem as well as Dante's own role as a reader of other poets' texts all point to the idea of reading as an activity of the deepest significance and seriousness. The consequences of the text are never neutral, and we know from the vestibule of hell what Dante thinks about neutrality. Yet we each work out our own relation to the demands of this unique text with its extraordinary eschatological claims. Giovanni Papini began his *Dante vivo* with the assertion that no one could truly understand Dante who was not a Catholic, a poet, and a Florentine.[4] But almost the opposite position might be argued from the current popularity of the *Divine Comedy*. The further we get from the poem's specifically medieval dimension, the more available it becomes in poetic terms. For the true subject of the *Divine Comedy* is not a philosophy or a theology; in the deepest sense the subject of the poem is the *act* of discovering and creating meaning in life and in art. The historical reality of Dante's Italy was as bitter as that of any country on the edge of constant civil war, and the Middle Ages were not only a time of extraordinary cultural achievement but also, as Yeats said, a time in which people went "on their knees or on all fours." The poem is not simply a synthesis of medieval cultural assumptions (although it is inconceivable without them); it is rather the unique and precarious achievement of Dante, a man whose life denied him the possibilities of order and justice for which he yearned and which he embodied forever in the most complex and finally affirmative of poems. The *Divine Comedy* is conservative politically and theologically but radical in its poetic daring and in its polemical insistence on the role of poetry in searching for and conveying the highest truths. Teaching it is a great privilege and a continuing source of joy.

Notes

[1] John Freccero, "*Paradiso* X: The Dance of the Stars," *Dante Studies*, 86 (1968), 85–111.

[2] Cited in Frank Kermode, *The Genesis of Secrecy: On the Interpretation of Narrative* (Cambridge: Harvard Univ. Press, 1979), p. 18.

[3] Giorgio Padoan, "Dante di fronte all'umanesimo letterario," in *Il pio Enea, l'empio Ulisse: Tradizione classica e intendimento medievale in Dante* (Ravenna: Longo, 1977), esp. pp. 27–29.

[4] Giovanni Papini, *Dante vivo* (Florence: Libreria Editrice Fiorentina, 1933), p. 7.

AN ARCHETYPAL APPROACH TO TEACHING THE *DIVINE COMEDY*

Gaetano Cipolla

Establishing a set of objectives for a course implies a univocal line of thinking that presupposes mastery of the subject. Although I have taught the *Divine Comedy* many times, I cannot claim such mastery. Teaching Dante is always a learning experience that I approach with a sense of humility as well as with a sense of expectation. For this reason, I can offer only some partial conclusions that have guided me in presenting this poem to undergraduates.

Dante is an essential poet. His *Divine Comedy* speaks to us of the timeless aspects of our lives, of all those things that really matter: love and hate, evil and goodness, free will and destiny, the fear of death and the hope of salvation, justice, and alienation. In the final analysis, the *Divine Comedy* is the embodiment of Dante's response to the challenges of his age; it transcends what is time-bound and embraces what is timeless and universal. I am reminded of a statement by Gianfranco Contini explaining the modernity of Petrarch's language. The Italian scholar claims that Petrarch's language is our own because "he surrounded himself with a circle of inevitable and eternal objects, rescued from the mutability of history."[1] While we cannot claim the same for Dante's language, we can certainly accept the latter part of Contini's statement as an accurate definition of Dante's craft. Dante, in fact, did rescue his characters from the mutability of history, placing them in a realm that is measured to the beat of eternity. Had it been otherwise, the *Divine Comedy* would have lost its appeal a long time ago.

In my presentation of Dante's work, I try to stress that he is not so much a poet of an age separated from us by a mountain of centuries but a poet who reaches through those centuries with a message that is both valid and timely. I try to make this point by stressing that the Middle Ages—a period of tremendous social, religious, and political upheaval, of great insecurity, and of continuous and devastating wars— were not so unlike our own age and by translating, if that is the correct term, Dante's experiences into the language and realities of the twentieth century. Dante's adoption of the allegorical mode was a brilliant piece of strategy that assured the validity of his work for all times.

In view of what I have said, and keeping in mind Dorothy Sayers' statement that "a great poetical image is much more than the sum of its interpretations,"[2] I will address myself to a specific approach that has proved quite effective in demonstrating the universality of Dante's poetry: the archetypal approach. Naturally, I do not use this approach to the exclusion of others. Indeed, it would be useful to remember Leslie Fiedler's caveat that "it is just as ridiculous to attempt the evaluation of a work of art purely in formal terms . . . as it would be to evaluate it purely in terms of the 'marvelous' or archetypal."[3]

A few considerations must be weighed before attempting an archetypal reading of the *Divine Comedy*. Chief among these are the interest and preparation of the teacher. Archetypal criticism will undoubtedly take him or her away from prepared fields into such areas as depth psychology, mythology, and anthropology, and the teacher must be well grounded in such fields. Other factors to consider are students' preparation, background, and interests. While not absolutely essential, it is desirable that students be conversant with such subjects; it could be disheartening, for example, to discover, while discussing the psychological implications of the myth of Theseus in their relation to Dante's journey, that many students have never heard of Theseus. Such things are discouraging, but they need not be fatal to the approach, for the onus of archetypal criticism rests principally on the teacher's shoulders. Just as in Jungian analysis the interpretation of the archetypal contents of a patient's dream rests with the analyst, in archetypal analysis the practitioner is called on to provide a universal context for the work by offering parallels, analogies, and interpretations drawn from substantial knowledge of other disciplines. Naturally, students should be encouraged to provide additional contexts, and they usually do so from their own experiences and readings.

At this point it will be fruitful to describe some specific procedures. The initial situation of the *Inferno*, the first tercet, is discussed at some length. By use of a technique known as "amplification," the class is brought to grasp the universality of the situation and to perceive its symbolic and psychological significance. The technique, developed by Jung to analyze dream images and motifs, provides a meaningful context for the image by comparing it to similar ones from mythology, folklore, and literature. Such an approach is particularly appropriate for Dante since the situation he describes is clearly of an oneiric nature, as many early as well as modern commentators have noted.[4] The material that can be used for comparison is vast. Literary examples describing analogous situations can be found in the first chapter of Melville's *Moby Dick*, in Book XI of Homer's *Odyssey*, in Goethe's *Faust*, and in numerous other works. For my Italian classes I like to compare Dante's initial plight with that of the protagonist of Elio Vittorini's *Conversazione in Sicilia* (Milan: Bompiani, 1941). Analogous motifs from mythology and folklore can also be extremely useful. Because of the spontaneous association between the confusing "selva oscura" ("dark wood") and the labyrinth, I have found it worthwhile to discuss the myth of Theseus not only to discover the analogies between it and Dante's journey but also to establish the archetypal stages through which all heroes must pass in order to reach their objectives. The cycle of the hero myth, schematized by the German anthropologist Leo Frobenius (1873–1938), amplified by Joseph Campbell, and interpreted by Erich Neumann, is of basic importance in Jungian psychology.[5] The stadial evolution of the hero from spiritual death to rebirth and transformation can easily be applied to Dante's journey and is valid for mankind as well, since every person lives, albeit in a symbolic fashion, through the same stages in an individual process of maturation. At times, depending on the responses and interests of the class, I expand the concept of the "diritta via" ("straight way") with a discussion of the archetype of the Way, its association with the Pythagorean letter Y, and the symbolism of the left and of the right.

What emerges from the analysis of such disparate sources is instructive to students because it clearly demonstrates that Dante was writing on a symbolic level of a universal condition that is outside of time and therefore applicable to all human beings. Students realize that the condition Dante describes is that of a man who is totally cut off from the creative psychic energies of the self. He has lost all direction in his life. The awakening in the dark wood, which is analogous to entering a series of dark corridors or embarking on a night sea voyage, can be considered the typical starting point of the journey to the center of the self, which is what the *Divine Comedy* represents. The "selva oscura" is the first manifestation of what Jung called the Shadow—that part of the unconscious that holds unknown or little-known attributes and qualities of the ego—and corresponds to the first stage in the process of individuation, that is, to the conscious coming to terms with one's own inner center. The Shadow—the brother within, the dark and danger-ous aspect of the unconscious—must be confronted directly if the pro-cess of individuation is to continue. This explains why Dante cannot ascend to the mountain of purgatory directly from the dark wood. The evil within him must be faced, recognized, assimilated, and trans-formed: in the language of mythology, the dragon must be slain. Dante must come to terms with those energies that lurk in the dark wood in an undifferentiated form. Once the concept of the Shadow has been introduced, students have little difficulty recognizing the three beasts that bar Dante's way as a fragmentation, or a splitting, of the archetype into its various aspects to enable the ego to confront each of the aspects in a less fearful way.

Dante's journey through the realms of the dead conforms so pre-cisely with what has been learned through the analysis of the human psyche that if one did not know better, one could suspect that the *Divine Comedy* had been written in our time as a lyric rethinking of modern psychological theories, as Egidio Guidubaldi has put it.[6] The correspondences between the *Divine Comedy* and the structure of the journey to the self elaborated by Jung and his followers could not be greater than they are. The students have little difficulty in seeing through the complexities of the *Divine Comedy* and reducing them to the simplest and oldest story of humankind, that of a hero who embarks on a journey to find a treasure. He is aided on his way by helpful figures and thwarted by threatening figures. He meets many obstacles and proves himself against many tests. Finally, he achieves his goal and returns with the precious gift he has won. The story, translated into psychological terms, is that of a barren ego that, aided by projec-tions from its own unconscious, embodied in such archetypal figures as wise old men and helpful maidens, confronts the unconscious and liberates the psychic energies that lie therein.

The characters that take part in Dante's journey can be seen as embodiments of the same archetypes that are activated in the adven-ture of the heroes. Vergil, as well as the other paternal figures, may be considered an embodiment of the archetype of the wise old man. Such figures, concerned with reason, the spirit, and the laws and institutions of society, frequently appear at the side of the seeker. Beatrice and the other helpful feminine figures are manifestations of the archetype "anima," whose alliance with the world of the spirit makes it possible for the seeker to confront the devouring, feminine aspect of the unconscious. Egidio Guidubaldi regards the archetypes of the *Divine Comedy* grouped in a triad of symbols, as follows (p. 346; the translation is my own):

1. Symbols of evil (gathered around the archetype of the Shadow)
2. Symbols of purification (centered in the dynamism of the archetype "anima")
3. Symbols of the Divine (distributed along the sapiential itinerary that begins with the archetype "wise old man")

Given the scope of this essay, it is difficult to treat the subject in greater detail, although much more needs to be said about each of the archetypes mentioned. To say that Beatrice is a projection of the unconscious, feminine side of Dante's personality would not be very interesting unless the characteristic features of the archetype and Dante's treatment of them were also discussed. It would be more meaningful, I think, to discuss Beatrice, as Maud Bodkin did in her *Archetypal Patterns in Poetry*,[7] as one aspect of Dante's relation to the feminine and to see how other female figures—Francesca, for example—are treated. And it would not be sufficient to equate Dante's celestial rose with the archetypal symbol of the self and of God, the mandala. It would be more rewarding to discuss it together with the numerous other manifestations of the divine that in Dante take the shape of mandalas.

I cannot conclude this brief discussion without mentioning another aspect of the archetypes that finds confirmation in the *Divine Comedy*. Every archetype embodied in symbols is two-faced; that is, it can be interpreted in a negative or positive fashion depending on the context in which the ego experiences it. It is remarkable that many of the archetypal images that appear as negative and threatening in the *Inferno* reappear in the other realms with positive connotations. The "selva oscura" of *Inferno* I, which caused Dante so much anguish, reappears as the "antica selva" of the Earthly Paradise. The sea of the unconscious that threatened to swallow Dante at the beginning of his journey has undergone a transformation in *Purgatorio* I. Dante no longer looks on it with dread; instead, he is able to gaze calmly and peacefully at the "tremolar della marina" ("trembling of the sea"). That "piaggia deserta" ("desert strand") of *Inferno* I, which calls to mind the archetypal experience of the wilderness—Adam and Eve ejected from the Earthly Paradise, Cain's wanderings, Dante's own exile—has become in the *Purgatorio* a lonely but peaceful "solingo piano" ("solitary plain"). The river Acheron, on whose shores the souls are amassed like leaves in autumn, reemerges as the purgatorial river whose shores are "dipinte di mirabil primavera" ("painted with marvelous spring"), reflecting the transformation from an autumnal, death-like landscape of the mind into one of spring and rebirth. These are only a few of the archetypal correspondences whose dynamism mirrors the stages of Dante's journey to the self.

An additional tool in the examination of the archetypal content of the *Divine Comedy* can be found in drawings and pictures, which psychologists call "constants of the unconscious." I am referring to the vast number of drawings and paintings that have been produced by people whose unconscious mind has been stimulated through various means. Many of these can be seen in C. G. Jung's *Man and His Symbols*.[8] Such works show a remarkable similarity to some of Dante's images and can be very illuminating to a class.

The teacher to whom these remarks are addressed will have to decide whether the results justify the long research. It seems to me, however, that the archetypal content, which is so pervasive in Dante's poem, cannot be ignored.

Notes

[1] Gianfranco Contini, Introd., *Canzoniere*, by Francesco Petrarca (Turin: Einaudi, 1964), p. xvi.

[2] Dorothy Sayers, Introd., *Hell*, Vol. I of *The Comedy of Dante Alighieri* (Baltimore: Penguin, 1949), p. 19.

[3] Leslie Fiedler, "Archetype and Signature," in *Symbol and Myth in Modern Literature*, ed. F. Parvin Sharpless (Rochelle Park, N.J.: Hayden, 1976), p. 42.

[4] Antonino Pagliaro, "Il proemio del poema sacro," in *Lectura Dantis Mystica*, Atti della Settimana Dantesca, Gressoney, 28 July–3 Aug. 1968 (Florence: Olschki, 1969), pp. 3–28.

⁵ Joseph Campbell, *The Hero with a Thousand Faces* (Princeton: Princeton Univ. Press, 1967); Erich Neumann, *The Origins and History of Consciousness*, trans. R. F. C. Hull, Bollingen Series, 47 (Princeton: Princeton Univ. Press, 1954).

⁶ Egidio Guidubaldi, "Dalla 'selva oscura' alla 'Candida rosa,' " in *Lectura Dantis Mystica*, Atti della Settimana Dantesca, Gressoney, 28 July–3 Aug. 1968 (Florence: Olschki, 1969), pp. 317–72.

⁷ Maud Bodkin, *Archetypal Patterns in Poetry* (1934; rpt. New York: Oxford Univ. Press, 1971).

⁸ Carl Gustav Jung, ed., *Man and His Symbols* (New York: Dell, 1968).

A COMPARATIVE APPROACH TO TEACHING THE *DIVINE COMEDY*

Marie Giuriceo

The unit on Dante that I describe is included in Landmarks of European Literature, a course offered by the Department of Comparative Literature at Brooklyn College. The catalog lists the course as follows:

> Introduction to principal themes, concerns, and values of European literature exemplified in such works as a courtly romance, Dante's *Divine Comedy*, Cervantes' *Don Quixote*, Racine's *Phèdre*, Voltaire's *Candide*, and Goethe's *Faust*. Interrelationship of national literatures through comparison of significant authors, ideas, and literary types in different ages or cultures.

Other works that may be included are Rabelais's *Gargantua and Pantagruel* (Books I and II), Corneille's *The Cid*, and Molière's *Tartuffe* or *The Misanthrope*. I choose to include all three in my syllabus. Although the catalog description cites the *Divine Comedy*, I concentrate on the *Inferno*, making numerous interconnections to show how the three canticles form a unity of experience and of design. To do less, I believe, would falsify Dante's artistic intent and achievement. I devote nine 50-minute class periods (or the equivalent) to Dante, two more than recommended. Students from the college at large take the

94

course, either to meet a requirement or as a free elective, at different points in their college careers.

In teaching Landmarks of European Literature, we seek to apply a comparative approach to the study of selected classics. From the opening session through the final examination, I never allow my students to lose sight of our approach. During the first meeting I define comparative literature and explain that we study each landmark as representing a period, as an example of a specific genre, from the points of view of themes, motifs, and types, and finally, in terms of literary relations.

I have four objectives in teaching the unit on Dante: (1) to present the *Divine Comedy* within its broad cultural context, not only as a reflection of the *Zeitgeist* of the Middle Ages but also as a literary *summa* that brings to a climax the cultural achievements of the Middle Ages and serves as a beacon for a new age, the Renaissance; (2) to engage in careful textual analysis of the *Inferno* in order to perceive its content and form as a unit and as an integral part of the *Divine Comedy*, to comprehend the *Divine Comedy* as a new stage of development in the epic genre, and to recognize its exceptional character; (3) to study the *Divine Comedy* from the point of view of themes, motifs, and types; (4) to consider the *Divine Comedy* in terms of literary relations, with regard to works that have influenced it or that it has influenced, in terms of meaningful comparisons, in relation to the problem of translation, and in connection with other disciplines—art, music, philosophy, theology, psychology, and history. It may be argued that it is impossible to accomplish such vast objectives in so limited a period of time. My response would be that accomplishing them is precisely the challenge posed by the course. Granted that it is not possible to achieve all four objectives completely, I know on the basis of long experience that it is possible to offer an enriching comparative experience if the instructor orchestrates the various parts of the course carefully.

How, then, do I go about accomplishing my goals? Although my unit on Dante lasts no longer than three weeks, I am painstakingly preparing for it in all preceding units. In the beginning of the semester I provide the medieval context necessary for understanding Gottfried's *Tristan* and Dante's *Divine Comedy*. To fill the gap in many students' knowledge of late antiquity and the Middle Ages, I distribute chronological and background handouts. The chronological sheets situate historical, literary, artistic, and musical events from A.D. 1 through the nineteenth century, and I ask my students to read them through the thirteenth century for purposes of reference. The background sheets outline historical and cultural events under topical headings from the first through the thirteenth century. I also devote a class period to showing slides of famous architectural monuments: Sant' Apollinare in Classe, Sant' Apollinare Nuovo, and San Vitale in Ravenna; Hagia Sophia in Constantinople; Charlemagne's chapel at Aix-la-Chapelle; Romanesque fortresses and churches; and Gothic cathedrals—all to illustrate successive stages in medieval history.

Next I treat certain literary developments of the Middle Ages: the heroic epic, the courtly lyric, and the courtly epic. In treating the courtly epic, I concentrate on its culmination in the epics of Chrétien de Troyes, singling out *Yvain* for its treatment of the quester theme. With this preparation, we proceed to the first assigned work of the semester, Gottfried von Strassburg's *Tristan*.

When we are nearing the completion of *Tristan*, I distribute my Dante handouts, which consist of background material on the life of Dante and the political scene in Florence, a statement on the scheme and argument of the *Divine Comedy*, and diagrams of the *Divine Comedy*, two for each canticle. For the first meeting on Dante I make the following assignment: review the background sheets on the Middle Ages, situate Dante on the chronological sheets, read the Dante handouts, begin reading the *Inferno*, at least through Canto X. I also ask students to ponder the following questions: How does the *Divine Comedy* reflect the *Zeitgeist* of the Middle Ages? What similarities do you see between the *Divine Comedy* and prior literary developments or prior works of literature? In particular, what specific connection can you make between the *Inferno* and Chrétien's *Yvain* and Gottfried's *Tristan*?

At our first session on Dante, I initiate discussion immediately on the assigned questions. At the conclusion of what is usually a broadly ranging exchange, I describe our discussion as exploratory and tentative and explain that I want it to start their thinking along comparative lines. I then present my four comparative objectives to guide subsequent discussions. My pedagogical techniques are a combination of lecture and class discussion, with an emphasis on the latter. I firmly believe in the question technique to initiate and develop class discussion. I know that the dynamic exchange between instructor and students exploring the text together makes an exciting class. Students frequently contribute new slants or fresh insights and occasionally make moving observations.

Since we read the *Inferno* in translation, I feel it incumbent on me to expatiate on the matter of translation. I begin by explaining that I chose the Sinclair edition for them because it is bilingual and provides extensive commentary. To compensate for its prosaic quality, however,

I urge them to read concurrently the Ciardi or Musa translation for its poetic qualities. In addition, after reminding them of the comparatist's natural interest in translation, I attempt to convey general problems confronting the translator and specific problems confronting the translator of the *Divine Comedy*.

The class is now ready to go to the text. I begin by reading aloud in Italian the opening passage of Canto I, asking any students who know Italian to take part. I comment about the splendid orchestration of the canto and the sound of the individual tercets. Then we begin our careful elucidation of Canto I, an explication that is imperative, since the canto serves as the prologue or overture to the entire epic. I solicit student commentary on the literal level of meaning: Dante's persona, setting, atmosphere, time, sequence of events leading up to Dante's encounter with Vergil, and finally the exchange between the two. We then examine the canto's complex allegory, emphasizing the seminal themes and images of the total work that emerge from it. I explain Dante's method of presenting allegory on three levels, which, with the literal level, give us the four senses of meaning traditional in medieval usage. Beyond matters of content, we explore formal matters: narrative, dramatic, and lyric modes of composition; allegorical techniques; introduction of first person narrative into epic form; structure and function of terza rima; method of character delineation; and nature of diction and imagery.

In commenting on the *Purgatorio* and the *Paradiso*, I describe the individual character of their kingdoms, as well as patterns picked up from the *Inferno* and woven through them, which give the epic its total unity of design. I also recount the dramatic peaks in both. From the *Purgatorio*, I describe the culmination of Dante's tutelage under Vergil and the commencement in the Earthly Paradise of his guidance from Beatrice. From the *Paradiso*, there is but one experience I transmit: Dante's supreme experience, his vision of the triune face of God. In doing so, I offer no commentary. I merely read the final passage of the canticle, which ends, as we all know, with the verses evoking the concluding lines of the first two canticles: "but now my desire and will, like a wheel that spins with even motion, were revolved by the Love that moves the sun and the other stars."

While it may appear that in my presentation of the *Divine Comedy* I concentrate on my second comparative objective—seeing the work's unity of form and content, as well as its emergence as a new form of epic—I am, nevertheless, concurrently interweaving the other objectives. With regard to the first, I am simultaneously showing the *Divine Comedy* as representing the Middle Ages in its view of the physical world, the Christian ethical system, and historical and political reality. I also describe it as a beacon for the Renaissance in its use of the vernacular, emphasis on individual personality, appropriation of the subject matter of antiquity, and spirit of intellectual inquiry. I single out the Brunetto Latini and Ulysses episodes as heralds of the new spirit of the Renaissance.

With regard to the third, from the mine of doctrinal, ethical, mythical, legendary, historical, political, and literary themes that inform the *Divine Comedy*, I choose to emphasize existential themes, such as quest, conversion, love, friendship, *Bildung*, reason, freedom, and suicide, not only because they are seminal themes in the epic but because their reappearance in other works of the semester offers infinite possibilities for fruitful comparison. I also trace the pattern of such significant motifs as woods, city, garden, hill, valley, stars, flame, rose, journey, Hebrew, and Roman. I explain the emergence of types from Dante's sharply etched portraits: Vergil, the type of human wisdom; Beatrice, spiritual love or the eternally feminine; Francesca, passionate love or earthly woman; Farinata, political commitment or magnanimity of spirit; Ulysses, insatiable thirst for knowledge; and Gianni Schicchi, false impersonation.

With regard to the fourth objective, I first discuss literary influence on Dante: the extent and depth of the presence of Vergil's writings, Dante's purposeful adaptation of the quester and love themes from the courtly epic, and his use of motifs and commonplaces from Provençal and Stilnovist lyric. Through our study of influences, we discover that Dante's adaptations are never sterile imitations but, rather, imaginative transformations. In studying Canto XXVI of the *Inferno* we compare Dante's treatment of Ulysses with Homer's and Vergil's treatment and also discuss the passage's strong influence on Tennyson's "Ulysses" and its possible impact on Joyce's *Ulysses*.

After my remarks on the *Paradiso*, I conclude with a summation of each of my objectives. I observe that the *Divine Comedy*, the first Christian epic, was a work of exceptional character: an encyclopedia, a chronicle of the soul, a vision, a *summa* that transfigures all literary forms known to Dante, a literary monument that corresponds to a Gothic cathedral in terms of its architectonic synthesis. I point out that as an attempt to conserve the values of the Middle Ages, it did not succeed, but its multifaceted humanism established Dante in the vanguard of the Renaissance. I remark that as we study other writers in the course, particularly Rabelais and Goethe, we shall discover exciting grounds for comparison with Dante.

An indispensable goal of my summation is to convey some sense of

Dante's influence beyond the purview of our course. In doing so, I am interested not in offering arid data but in informing students of the varied ways in which Dante nurtured the imagination of subsequent writers. I cite Boccaccio in the *Decameron* as having received the impulse for realistically representing a multifarious world, contemporary Italy in the fourteenth century, after the manner of Dante's creation of a richly diverse world in the *Divine Comedy;* Chaucer's adaptation of the Ugolino story in the *Monk's Tale;* parallels between the *Divine Comedy* and Milton's *Paradise Lost.* By way of demonstrating the phenomenal burst of Dante's influence in the romantic period, I adduce Byron's "Francesca da Rimini," Browning's "Sordello," as well as Tennyson's "Ulysses" and the Pre-Raphaelite enthusiasm for him. Moving beyond England, I mention the influence of Dante on nineteenth-century French writers, on Baudelaire in his theory of correspondences and on Balzac in his conception of the *comédie humaine* as an encyclopedic treatment of the very human world of nineteenth-century France. I single out Balzac's presentation in *Père Goriot* of the "real" education of Eugène de Rastignac by his "father" mentors in contrast to the "ideal" education of Dante under the guidance of his spiritual father Vergil. Eugène's education recalls that of Julien Sorel in *The Red and the Black* and the succession of father figures in his life. I suggest comparisons between Flaubert's Madame Bovary and Francesca da Rimini, who was similarly beguiled by romantic literature, and I indicate the affinities of Francesca and Emma with Tolstoy's Anna Karenina in their adulterous affairs. I also discourse on the American writers attracted to Dante—Lowell, Longfellow, Melville, Hawthorne, and possibly Poe. I mention Longfellow's establishment of the long tradition of Dante studies at Harvard.

I conclude my discussion of literary influence by indicating the continuing interest in Dante in the twentieth century among poets as well as novelists. I cite influence on poets such as Paul Claudel and Eugenio Montale in Europe and Ezra Pound, T. S. Eliot, Wallace Stevens, Stephen Crane, and Robert Lowell in America. I also contend that novelists such as Marcel Proust, Thomas Mann, and James Joyce learned many techniques from Dante for the construction of fictive worlds. It is possible to discern in *Remembrance of Things Past* some indebtedness of Proust to Dante in the use of circular and triangular structure, first person narrative, and optical imagery. In the Dedalus-Bloom relation in *Ulysses* and in the Castorp-Settembrini relation in *The Magic Mountain* we have modern examples of *Bildung* after the manner of the Dante-Vergil relation in the *Divine Comedy.* We may even argue for an ongoing dialectic with Dante in the minds of contemporary novelists upon observing that Thomas Merton entitles a work *The Seven Story Mountain,* evoking Dante's purgatory, that Sartre's *No Exit* and Camus's *The Fall* are modern versions of hell, and that Beckett configures Sordello and Belacqua in his trilogy *Molloy, Malone,* and *The Unnamable* to serve his purpose of demythologizing human existence.

I also show the influence of the *Divine Comedy* on the other arts, suggesting that students go to the music library and listen to recordings of Tchaikovsky's *Francesca da Rimini,* Puccini's *Gianni Schicchi,* and Liszt's *Dante Sonata* and *Dante Symphony.* I conclude by showing illustrations of the *Divine Comedy* by Botticelli, Domenico di Michelino, Ingres, Delacroix, Doré, and Blake, as well as a photograph of Carpeaux's sculpture of Ugolino and his sons, on display at the Metropolitan Museum of Art. I also suggest that students consider the possible influence of Dante on filmmakers, such as Fellini or Francis Ford Coppola in *Apocalypse Now.*

Because I emphasize the interrelations of the arts, students occasionally submit artwork of their own accord. A few years ago a comparative literature major, who is also an artist, submitted a most ambitious project, illustrations of the *Inferno* and the *Purgatorio.* More recently, a student submitted an oil painting of Dante foiled by the beasts as he attempts to climb the hill of the dark wood. I also show these works to my class. At the conclusion of our unit, Dante leaves center stage, but our comparative approach ensures his many reappearances throughout the semester.

DIVINING THE *COMEDY:* DANTE AND UNDERGRADUATES

Philip J. Gallagher

Dante's *Divine Comedy* is the most challenging poem I have ever read or taught. Unlike other narratives it is rarely expository; instead, it dramatizes numerous episodes whose meaning the reader must educe in emulation of Vergil, of whom Dante says, "You are wise / and will grasp what my poor words can but suggest" (Ciardi, trans., *Inf.* II. 35–36), and after the fashion of the wayfarer himself, whose inferential skills are displayed when, having cited certain observations of the shade of Pope Adrian V, he remarks, "I took good note / of what its way of speaking did not hide" (*Purg.* XIX. 83–84). Taking "good note" is precisely the burden of the wayfarer and the reader alike, or, to use Dante's metaphor, "I set out food, but you yourself must feed!" (*Par.* X. 25).

In my experience, undergraduates typically are in no position to heed Dante's injunction. To enable them to do so, I urge upon them five interrelated but logically distinguishable exegetical rules of thumb: read the text grammatically, read it literally, grasp each episode in its immediate eschatological context, be on the lookout for significant episodic juxtapositions, and consider the poem comparatively as a quest epic. I implement these rules through well-ordered study questions, as illustrated in the following pages.

101

Read the Text Grammatically

To Dante, the beatitude of rational creatures consists primarily in an act of intellectual apprehension (*Par.* XXVIII. 106–11): hence the phrase "beatific vision" and Vergil's description of the damned as "souls who have lost the good of intellect" (*Inf.* III. 18). The same principle holds for Dante's readers: the first prerequisite of understanding is to discern what the verbal signs signify semantically—in and of themselves—and grammatically—in relation to the other semantic elements in their immediate syntactic environment. My point is obvious, but it can never be taken for granted, as I am reminded when generally superior students misread such difficult passages as *Purgatorio* XXVII. 136–38. Valid interpretation is impossible without first reading the text grammatically, and this tautology is the foundation of many of my study questions.

Read the Text Literally

In the letter to Can Grande, Dante (if we can believe that he wrote it) insists that the literal subject of the *Divine Comedy*, and the matrix from which its several meanings emerge, is the state of souls after death. The poet is first of all concerned with the ontological destiny of souls: as a wayfarer, Dante went into eschatology in the flesh and tells literally what he saw there. Since the demise of the cosmology of Ptolemy of Alexandria, on which the literal truth of Dante's journey is predicated, it is impossible to affirm Dante's geocentric universe (much less his bodily journey through it) and almost impossible to suspend our disbelief. Instead, the urge is to demythologize the *Divine Comedy*, to regard the journey as an allegory of the poets, a beautiful but incredible fable from under whose ephemeral surface may be salvaged some worthy spiritual truth. There are, assuredly, instances of such allegory in the poem: *Inferno* I, for example, takes place in an allegorical landscape; no less a literalist than Thomas Aquinas tells, and explicates, an allegory of Francis of Assisi and Lady Poverty (*Par.* XI. 43–75); and even Beatrice allegorizes when she tries to make Plato's *Timaeus* safe for orthodoxy (*Par.* IV. 49–63). But what is striking about these and similar instances is precisely that they stand out as exegetical anomalies. Even in the *Paradiso*, where, excepting Cantos XXX–XXXIII, Dante's literal journey through the spheres of the material universe is a gigantic accommodation arranged to make heaven intelligible to mortal apprehension, the poet encourages readers to rest in his accommodated words and images rather than to search for a nonliteral esoteric doctrine behind the (relative) simplicity of the text: "Let the example speak," he cries, "until God's grace / grants the pure spirit the [literal] experience" (*Par.* I. 71–72) of heaven itself. As if to underscore the point, Dante records from his own experience just such an error of interpretation as he would have his reader avoid: in the sphere of the moon he misapprehends the faces of the inconstant as reflected images and must be reminded by Beatrice not to search for reality beyond the great appearances of things (*Par.* III. 7–29).

I try to foster in my students a healthy respect for the literal by calling attention in my study questions to passages such as those just cited and also by inviting students to contemplate the more or less absurd consequences of reading certain passages allegorically. Two brief examples from the *Purgatorio* must suffice.

At *Purgatorio* XIII, on the cornice of envy, Dante reports almost offhandedly that "Vergil was walking by me down the ledge / on the side from which—because no parapet / circled the cliff—one might plunge off the edge" (ll. 79–81). This information is not without significance: the repentant sinners are blind and so must lean for support and safety against the inner face of the cliff (ll. 59–72); consequently, the wayfarer must tread the dangerous outside circumference of the mountain. Dante's recording the fact is an instance of poetic accuracy; it also compliments Vergil, whose habitual, selfless solicitude toward his charge has, a canticle ago, earned him the triple epithet, "my stay, my comfort, and my courage" (*Inf.* XVII. 89). Ignoring these relevant implications, and in response to a study question designed to elicit a figurative reading, a student said of lines 79–81: "Allegorically, the soul puts Reason between itself and a fall." He was, however, hard put to respond when I asked him why Dante's soul should require such a champion here, among the envious, as opposed, let us say, to below, among the proud; and when I pointed to the fact that the poet's real and present danger is, as he himself testifies, pride, not envy (*Purg.* XIII. 133–38), he had to admit that allegory, like pride, often goeth before a fall of its own.

My second example, which resembles the first, is taken from the cornice of lust. There purgative fire blasts the ledge from the inner wall, leaving for the itinerant wayfarers only a narrow passageway along the outer ledge. Thus beset by danger on two fronts, Vergil aptly cautions Dante: "In this place, it is clear, / we all must keep a tight rein on our eyes. / To take a false step would be easy here" (*Purg.* XXV. 118–20). Now in the context of lust, Vergil's warning involves a learned poetic witticism, it being an amorous convention that love enters through the eyes. But is he also warning Dante allegorically to beware of lust? One student thought so: "Reason must curb the sense of sight," he wrote, "lest ignoring Christ's injunction one fall into adultery unawares." I rebutted this interpretation by citing Dante's inability to heed Vergil's (tongue-in-cheek) advice, curious as he is to witness the fiery torments of the cornice (ll. 121–26). Then I asked, "Are we to believe, allegorically, that our poet, by looking into the fire, has adulterated himself by lusting after the lustful?"

By leading my students deliberately into the absurd consequences of certain allegorical assumptions, I try to disabuse them of the notion that poetic meaning is to be found by extracting generalized notions from concrete images. Indeed, the opposite seems more often to be true in the *Divine Comedy:* Dante incarnates the abstract, giving it a local habitation and a name in eschatological space. I urge this truth on my students by citing, for example, the avaricious who in *Purgatorio* XIX endlessly intone Psalm 118:25 (Vulgate). The biblical text reads "Down in the dust I lie prostrate," a figurative utterance, bespeaking a humble state of mind rather than a bodily configuration. But with an accuracy entirely Dantesque, the penitent souls of the fifth cornice alter the verse to conform to their otherworldly fate: " 'My soul cleaves to the dust' " (1.73), they cry, alluding at once to their disembodied state and to their literal doom, since, as the wayfarer has observed, these shades are a "people everywhere / lying outstretched and facedown on the ground" (ll. 71–72)—"biting the dust," as it were.

Grasp Each Episode in Its Immediate Eschatological Context

In the fifth subdivision of Malebolge Dante reluctantly (but perforce) commits himself to the care of ten demon cohorts of the Blacktalon Malacoda. Concerned over the decorum of so proceeding, the poet consoles himself by invoking an ancient proverb: "In church with saints; with stewpots in the tavern" (*Inf.* XXII. 14). Beyond this aphorism's obviously social orientation ("When in Rome . . .") lies an aesthetic corollary of singular importance for the *Divine Comedy:* the episodes of the poem are illuminated by observing precisely where they occur. Geography becomes, so to speak, a silent but infallible scholiast. Examples are legion: exhausted by his climb up antepurgatory, Dante rests—where else?—on the cornice of the indolent (*Purg.* IV. 46–54); the penitent shade of Hugh Capet, scrupulous now to avoid even the impression of this-worldly greed, declines Dante's offer to pray for his soul in exchange for information about the whip of avarice (*Purg.* XX. 34–42); and Statius delivers a learned disquisition on human reproduction as the pilgrims ascend to the cornice of the lustful (*Purg.* XXV. 37–78). To call the importance of geographical context to my students' attention I compose study questions such as "Account for the behavior of Cavalcante dei Cavalcanti (*Inf.* X. 52–72) in view of the fact that he espoused the materialist heresy of Epicureanism."

Be on the Lookout for Significant Episodic Juxtapositions

Like many a long narrative poem, the *Divine Comedy* must be read synchronically as well as diachronically: meaning is released when individual episodes are seen as having been deliberately juxtaposed. Is it not striking that both the carnal (*Inf.* V. 28–39) and the sodomites (*Inf.* XV. 37–42) are forever on the move? Is not the pathetic suicide of Pier delle Vigne (*Inf.* XIII. 29–108) shorn of all pathos when judged in the light of Romeo da Villanova's heroic response (*Par.* VI. 127–43) to an adversity in all respects symmetrical with that which dogged delle Vigne? Consider how the destiny of the Emperor Trajan unfolds in Dante's epic; we see him first in a bas-relief that constitutes part of the whip of pride (*Purg.* X. 70–90). The panel depicts a widow seeking justice for her son, a justice Trajan promises to secure, but perhaps only through the projected good offices of his successor. The dissatisfied widow replies, "Can the good deed / another does grace him who shuns his own?" (ll. 86–87). Her rhetorical question implies a negative answer, designed as it is to secure an immediate redress of grievance. Yet it also resonates with other implications, for as *Paradiso* VII. 19–120 makes clear, the whole scheme of redemption through Christ is predicated on an affirmative response to just such a question as she asks. Moreover, in a providential irony lost on Trajan until after his death and obscured for Dante's reader until *Paradiso* XX. 43–48 and 94–117, it happens that Trajan, who as a pagan shunned his own ultimate good, was himself graced by the good deed of another, Pope Gregory I, in fact, whose ardent prayers for the damned emperor actually secured his postmortem release from hell into beatitude.

Such bewildering complexities can be introduced to the undergraduate in the form of leading questions, such as "Explain *Inferno* XV. 91–99, especially lines 97–99, in the light of *Inferno* VII. 67–96"; and "Account for Vergil's behavior at *Purgatorio* XXI. 130–37 in the light of *Purgatorio* VII. 1–15 and XIX. 130–41."

Consider the Poem Comparatively as a Quest Epic

Toward the end of *Inferno* XX, Vergil, ever the willing pedagogue, identifies for the inquisitive Dante the shade of a Greek fortune-teller: "He is Eurpylus [says Vergil, matter-of-factly]. I sing him somewhere / in my High Tragedy; you will know the place / who know the whole of it" (ll. 112–14). Apart from acknowledging (and so complimenting) the wayfarer's intimate familiarity with the *Aeneid*, Vergil implies that anyone essaying to comprehend the *Divine Comedy* must likewise know the whole of the Roman epic and, through it, the Homeric tradition. The reader who approaches Dante without prior immersion in its classical sources will perhaps be able to appreciate the extraordinary typological expropriation by which the whole of Roman history as rehearsed in the *Aeneid* is made, at *Inferno* II. 13–30, to prefigure and providentially to prepare for the birth of Christ and the Christian dispensation. Nor will such a reader be unduly disoriented by, for example, Dante's criticism of Vergil for tracing Dido's insane assignation with Aeneas in Book IV of the *Aeneid* to the irresistible impulsions of Venus (*Par.* VIII. 1–9). But how is the unlearned reader to cope with other, more problematical and subterranean, allusions? At *Inferno* IX. 40–41, Dante remarks appositely but also *en passant* that "My Master . . . well knew / the handmaids [Erinyes] of the Queen of Woe [Proserpine]." The reader who knows only that the Erinyes are agents of divine retribution will have failed to grasp the import and the justice of Dante's exact observation: the poet has in mind the splendidly orchestrated description in *Aeneid* VII of Juno haling the Fury Alecto from the underworld to foment enmity between Aeneas and King Latinus: Vergil indeed "well knew" the handmaid of Proserpine—and with a literal vengeance! Or again: the bas-reliefs of the whip of pride are extraordinary in that they depict characters who seem to be about to speak words that Dante is miraculously able to hear and record (*Purg.* X. 25–96). When the poet defers to the genius of the Divine Artist who "produced that 'visible speaking' [,] / new to us, because not found below" (ll. 92–93), readers familiar with the murals that adorn the temple of Juno in *Aeneid* I, and with the exquisite shield that Aeneas hoists in Book VIII—such readers, and only such readers, will grasp Dante's intention here, where pride is purged, to mock the vainglorious artistic asseverations of his pagan predecessors.

Since the *Inferno* is patterned on the descent of Aeneas (and Odysseus) to the underworld and since Dante frames his ascent to paradise by twice comparing it to the voyage of Jason and the Argonauts (*Par.* II. 1–18 and XXXIII. 94–97), I teach the *Divine Comedy* as the *terminus ad quem* in a two-semester survey course involving also the *Odyssey*, the *Aeneid*, and the *Argonautica* of Apollonius Rhodius. If it be asked why I consider these works at the expense, say, of Aquinas' *Summa Theologica*, I respond, first, that they are infinitely more accessible to the undergraduate than Saint Thomas is and, second, that the comparative analysis of the *Divine Comedy* in the light of its epic predecessors is interpretively so fruitful as amply to justify the undertaking. My point is illustrated by *Inferno* XXVI. 43–131.

At issue there is the fate of Ulysses, whom Dante places among the evil counselors. How did he get there? Having escaped from Circe and in utter disregard of father, wife, and son, he arrogantly deluded his shipmates into pursuing forbidden experiences beyond the Straits of Gibraltar and into the southern hemisphere. When, after a five-month voyage, Ulysses approached Mount Purgatory, God sent a squall to destroy his ship, kill its crew, and expedite the speedy descent of their captain into the eighth circle of hell. Now what transforms this exemplum of Promethean overreaching into a work of art is precisely Dante's stunning manipulation of Homeric materials. How would Homer react to Dante's treatment of Ulysses? He would affirm, with Dante, that after escaping from Circe, Odysseus explored uncharted waters, but he would find it contrary to Odysseus' natural inclination (which is always homeward), in obedient submission to the expressed will of the gods (*Odyssey* X. 482–93). He would affirm with Dante that after departing from Circe, Odysseus descended into hell, but he would view him as a suppliant, not a sinner, seeking protocols pertinent to a speedy homecoming (*Odyssey* XI. 90–117), not "experience of the world beyond the sun" (*Inf.* XXVI. 109). He would affirm, with Dante, that Odysseus journeyed into eschatology, but he would deny that the man of many turns failed to return.

The reader who would be at home in Dante's cosmos must be competent to peruse the *Divine Comedy* from the perspective of a Homer or a Vergil. In the interest of cultivating such readers, I challenge my students with study questions like "Evaluate Dante's dream of Sirena (*Purg.* XIX. 1–33) in the light of *Odyssey* XII. 39–54 and 158–200" and "Evaluate *Purgatorio* XVIII. 136–38, in the light of *Aeneid* V. 604–799." Such questions are often as difficult to write as they are to answer, but without doubt they help teachers to teach and students to learn. I know from experience.

SELECTED COURSES AND UNITS ON DANTE: PEDAGOGICAL STRATEGIES

PARADISO AND THE ORIENT IN FLINT, MICHIGAN

Judith Kollmann

The University of Michigan at Flint is very different from its parent institution at Ann Arbor. A relatively new school of some thirty-nine hundred students, it is located in the inner city of Flint and is a commuter institution serving the surrounding city and county. Not surprisingly, the students are typical of the industrial Midwest. Many cannot read accurately and most cannot write critically, but this is a matter of a lack of acquired skills and not a lack of intelligence. Most are from the middle class, many are white, some are black, and a few are Chicano or American Indian. As a rule they are bright, and sometimes gifted. They are not, as yet, jaded or blasé about life or knowledge, and so, although they come seeking careers and social position, sometimes they leave having found the joy of intellectual pursuit.

Teaching them the *Divine Comedy* is at once a challenge and a delight, so much so, in fact, that I have taught one volume or other of the *Divine Comedy* at every undergraduate level. I have used the *Inferno* for freshman composition as well as for an upper-division course in medieval literature, and the *Paradiso* (and sometimes the *Inferno* or the *Purgatorio* as well) for a sophomore course ambitiously titled The Medieval World of Infinite Variety. It is this course, and the purposes for which the *Divine Comedy* is employed in it, that is the topic of the present paper.

Sophomore courses at the University of Michigan at Flint are intended to accomplish a variety of objectives, principally to introduce the students to the rich cultural heritage of the world and the relevance of other literatures. Infinite Variety was designed to introduce the students to Mediterranean, Near Eastern, and Far Eastern literature written from approximately A.D. 700 to 1350 and was also intended to deal with history, culture, and intellectual developments. Although several courses were available at the Flint campus concerning the European Middle Ages and the more modern East, nothing was available regarding Eastern civilizations flourishing at the time of the European Middle Ages, although those centuries are among the richest in the history of human development.

The content of the course has varied slightly each time it has been offered, owing in part to the availability of reliable translations and in part to the need to select topics carefully. The material is vast and can easily get out of hand, dissolving into a superficial survey. The literature has been selected on the basis of three criteria: first, for its intrinsic excellence; second, for its significance in the culture that it represents; third, for its relation to literature of other cultures. The course seeks to avoid a chronological survey of each culture from the eighth through the fourteenth century and to offer instead a representative cross-sectional slice of what was happening in different parts of the world while Europe was hatching the Middle Ages.

The course, organized geographically and thematically, begins with the *Paradiso* as the representative of the Western world. At one time I used the *Song of Roland* and the *Cid*, but these proved too limited in scope. On another occasion I used the entire *Divine Comedy*, but this was too large and unwieldy. The class first spends four weeks of a fourteen-week semester on Western literature and thought and then moves to Islamic literature, spending three weeks discussing the basic precepts of Muslim faith and reading a number of selections from the *Koran* before proceeding to secular Persian and Arabic prose and poetry. The third unit, of two weeks, deals with either India's Kannadan worshipers of Siva (who produced notable poetry during the tenth through the twelfth century) or with the Jewish poets of Spain (who flourished from the tenth through the thirteenth century during the Islamic occupation). The fourth unit, of $2\frac{1}{2}$ weeks, is concerned with the T'ang poets of China, while the fifth and final unit (also $2\frac{1}{2}$ weeks) studies Japan through its acknowledged masterpiece, Lady Murasaki's *Tale of Genji* (ca. 1000). Thus Infinite Variety tries to show the students something of the beauty and wealth of human experience.

In order to provide a firm basis for the comparison and contrast of cultures, however, it is necessary to understand one's own. Experience has shown that our students have little understanding of the present and still less of the past. For this reason, the *Divine Comedy* fulfills an essential function that no other work of medieval literature can perform as adequately: definition. It contains nearly everything illustrative of medieval European culture and thought, with the exception of the chivalric ideal. The abundance of the *Divine Comedy* is overwhelming: medieval Christianity developed to its apogee in mystic vision; attitudes toward friendship, women, love, politics, war, ethics, time, infinity, the scheme of the universe and our place within it; philosophy, theology, science, geography, history. At once introspective and outwardly directed, the breadth of vision of the *Divine Comedy,* and especially of the *Paradiso,* defines the best of medieval Western art and also offers a wealth of effective comparison and contrast to anything presented in the Eastern literatures.

The great drawback, of course, is the difficulty of the text of the *Paradiso,* offering, as it does, abstract theological or philosophical concepts in language that appears at times more complex than the ideas it tries to explain. What can be done to help the students over this chief difficulty in using this canticle? Since this is a sophomore course, I look not so much for a thorough understanding and mastery of Dante's text as for an *appreciation* of it. I want these students to enjoy what they are doing and to become excited by Dante's art and his ideas. To add to the difficulties, the course is well attended, precluding the possibility of class discussion. Therefore, I have developed a style of lecture that does a lot of explaining while it proceeds (as I warn students) by means of digressions, many anecdotes, interesting trivia. Frequently the semester becomes an intellectual game: through their questions the students try to see how long they can entice me off the scheduled topic. My challenge is to use these same questions to get back to the mainstream. It's all in good sportsmanship and creates a situation such that, when we get into something as intellectually demanding as the *Divine Comedy,* the students are receptive and even interested. In the process, I take good care to explain the Middle Ages, Christianity (experience has shown that many fundamentalist as well as Catholic students often understand neither their own religious traditions nor the basic factors that all Christian sects share in common), and the structure of the *Divine Comedy.* But I do not try to explain the entire poem. Instead, I select one or two themes that will not only make the work as a whole more intelligible to them but also provide a means of unifying the rest of the course.

The possibilities are multiple; two themes that have lent themselves well to my purposes are passionate love and mysticism. The students are interested in eros and ecstasy. Dante's attitude toward passionate love offers a splendid insight into his sense of ethics and priorities that fascinates the students because it is not what they expect (what they expect is puritanic American mores), and therefore the subject of passionate love actually opens up the entire *Divine Comedy* for them. I point out that, in relation to the rest of hell and its inhabitants, Paolo and Francesca are not badly situated (of course this opening gambit provides a means for discussing Dante's concept of grave sin as the alienation of one person from another and the regression of individuals into themselves until the ultimate in egomania is reached at the bottom of the pit). The sin of eros is the last sin to be cleansed in purgatory and is therefore, by implication, the least of the great sins. The position of the redeemed lovers, in the sphere of the third heaven, represents a considerable "improvement" over the people who couldn't stick with a good plan or over those who had been too busy to bother with religion. It is then a fairly simple thing to elaborate on what Dante meant by a fully developed, rightful love for human beings and God as we proceed through the *Paradiso*. With this as the paradigm for Western Christian attitudes toward love, the course continues to explore the theme until, as the students proceed further and further away from the Western world and are exposed to different attitudes toward human relations, the final, and greatest, contrast is reached in the *Tale of Genji*, in which people use one another with consummate elegance, and ultimate value lies in aesthetic grace.

The second theme that I like to develop, because of its further bearing on Eastern literatures, is mysticism. Mysticism is a word that needs to be defined with care, in terms of both what it is and what it is *not* (that is, it is neither the occult nor any search for power). Considerable time (at least one or two class hours) is spent on this definition, as it is a key term for the rest of the semester. The emphasis is on mysticism as a universal psychological phenomenon experienced by individuals among all religious systems, and it is defined as the search for (and possibly the achievement of) a personal contact with divinity. The whole of the *Divine Comedy* records one man's search for God, of course, and the final verses of the *Paradiso* are the culmination of that search in sudden achievement:

> So strove I with that wonder—how to fit
> The image to the sphere; so sought to see
> How it maintained the point of rest in it.

> Thither my own wings could not carry me,
> But that a flash my understanding clove,
> Whence its desire came to it suddenly.

> High phantasy lost power and here broke off;
> Yet, as a wheel moves smoothly, free from jars,
> My will and my desire were turned by love,
> The love that moves the sun and the other stars.
> (*Par.* XXXIII. 136–45)[1]

For this course, these lines prove not only a summation of Western religious expression but a launching point into Islamic Sufism and the *vacanas* of the *Virasaiva* saints. The students are fascinated by the similarities and dissimilarities of Dante's lines to these by Rumi (1207–73), poet, Sufi, Persian, and near contemporary of Dante:

> This is Love: to fly heavenward,
> To rend, every instant, a hundred veils.
> The first moment, to renounce life;
> The last step, to fare without feet.
> To regard this world as invisible,
> Not to see what appears to one's self.
> "O heart," I said, "may it bless thee
> To have entered the circle of lovers,
> To look beyond the range of the eye,
> To penetrate the windings of the bosom!"[2]

Or to this vacana by Allana Prabhu:

> Looking for your light,
> I went out:
>
>> it was like the sudden dawn
>> of a million million suns,
>>
>> a ganglion of lightnings
>> for my wonder.
>
> O Lord of Caves,
> if you are light,
> there can be no metaphor.[3]

Beyond the reading materials and attendance at lectures, there are three requirements for the course: a midterm examination, a paper, and a final exam. The paper, which is fairly short (ten to twelve double-spaced, typed pages) is to be analytic in nature and requiring research. The examinations are designed to test not so much the students' grasp of details as their understanding of the characteristics of each culture and its literature. The midterm tests the students over Dante and Islamic literature; the first section of the final exam tests them over the remainder of the course, while the second part of the final, an essay question, encourages them to assess the materials of the entire course. Both the midterm and first part of the final consist of identification questions, some of which ask the students to recapitulate important passages from literature in terms of the culture that produced the work rather than by author or title.

By far the most important part of the final examination, however, is the second part, the essay that requires them to summarize the course analytically. But since students are often too tense to think clearly or write well during finals, I have tried to find ways of asking questions that may help them relax a bit. These alternatives may seem ridiculous, but they have produced a high percentage of good answers:

> One day, as you are preparing for the final exam in English 208, you are strolling along Saginaw Street. However, as your mind is concentrating on Tao, Confucius, Rumi, Siva, and the Shining Prince, to say nothing of the Empress Wu and Lady Murasaki Shikibu, you really aren't paying much attention to where you're going. As a consequence you step into an open manhole. While slowly swimming back to consciousness in Hurley Hospital you have the following vision:
>
> Dante is explaining his friendship with, and love of, Beatrice and Bernard to Li Po, Rumi, and Lady Murasaki. What do you think Dante would say, and what would be the response of each member of his audience?

The Medieval World of Infinite Variety was designed to introduce students to the wealth of human imagination and thought produced during six centuries on three continents. It has, I think, owed its sense of purpose and unity largely to Dante's *Divine Comedy*, not only because it offers a definition of Western medieval men and women but also because the wealth of its thematic interests offers any number of ways with which to give direction to the rest of the course. My own choices of "eros and ecstacy," the two extremes of love, simply span the interests of every culture.

In any case, the course appears to have been successful in its aims. Perhaps the best proof is that its students have often gone on to more specialized courses in medieval literature, in the Near and Far East, and even to independent study in the *Divine Comedy*.

Notes

[1] Dante Alighieri, *The Divine Comedy: Paradise*, trans. Dorothy Sayers and Barbara Reynolds (1962; rpt. Baltimore: Penguin, 1966), p. 347.

[2] James Kritzec, ed., *Anthology of Islamic Literature: From the Rise of Islam to Modern Times* (New York: Mentor, 1966), pp. 227–28.

[3] A. K. Ramanujan, trans., *Speaking of Siva* (Baltimore: Penguin, 1973), p. 168.

THE *PURGATORIO* AS A UNIT IN A MEDIEVAL LITERATURE COURSE

Elizabeth R. Hatcher

Although I occasionally teach a course devoted entirely to the *Divine Comedy*, my main experience in teaching the poem comes from use of the *Purgatorio* in a one-semester course on medieval literature offered within the university's English department. In the ten years since my department in its innocence entrusted me with teaching what was then a course called Middle English Literature, the course has developed into something of an exercise in *chutzpah*. I state the objectives in broad terms in order to give myself maximum flexibility in choice of works and approaches:

> Students should gain *knowledge* of the major genres and the outstanding authors and works of the medieval period. They should gain *understanding* of the aesthetic, philosophical, psychological, and spiritual principles that guided the creation of these works. They should increase their *skills* of reading, analysis, research, and writing by working with the cultural documents from this period and from published studies of them. They should develop *attitudes* of interest in the period, its literary works, and its contributions to the development of human culture. Their study of the dominant values of the period should

help them in their quest to clarify and define their own personal *values.*

Fixtures on the reading list are the *Consolation of Philosophy* by Boethius, the *Purgatorio, Piers Plowman, Sir Gawain* and the *Pearl,* some lyrics, and some readings in Sir Thomas Malory. Coming and going are such works as *Beowulf,* the *Song of Roland,* the *Romance of the Rose,* the *Vineland Sagas,* the *Cloud of Unknowing,* some non-Arthurian English romances, and *Mandeville's Travels.*

I suppose that the major peculiarities of the course are that it covers a thousand years and that although it is an English majors' period course, it covers a considerable body of non-English literature, including Dante. These characteristics are the result of my presuppositions both about the nature of the medieval period and about how best to meet the needs of the kinds of students who take the course.

First, is it not a bit cavalier to consider a whole millennium as a single period? As one who was, academically speaking, conceived in the Catholic schools, where students used to read about "Pope Hildebrand" (Gregory VII) in sixth grade, and weaned on Ernst Robert Curtius' *European Literature and the Latin Middle Ages,* and baptized into the Johns Hopkins tradition of the history of ideas, I view the medieval millennium (give or take a century) as a single entity; to be sure, it is not one bound by the unities of time, place, and action, but nonetheless it is a period comfortably marked off from those preceding and following it by characteristic concerns and attitudes. I tell the students that running through the literature we will read are the themes of the dream of empire, the quest for God, and the love of the world. These themes have proved both specific enough to give order and meaning to the readings and flexible enough not to interfere with the individuality and uniqueness of any particular work.

Starting with Boethius allows me to root the first of these themes in a sketch of the social and political vicissitudes of the late Roman Empire. I can then point out how later literature—the *Song of Roland,* the *Divine Comedy,* Arthurian material, *Piers Plowman*—reflects various forms of struggle or yearning for the establishment of a social order, an "empire" in the medieval Christian sense. Boethius is again the appropriate starting point for the other two themes. Boethius comes to terms with his own love of the world and all it has to offer by discovering that it is really an unintegrated quest for God. I then trace tensions and resolutions between and among these themes as they appear in later works. This discussion provides a splendid introduction to the *Purgatorio,* which in its early cantos emphasizes the theme of the

Exodus, of nostalgia following a passover from a world loved in and for itself to a world of directionality, of struggle upward, of moving from foreshadowing to foreshadowing toward an unmediated truth that seems forever out of reach. The Casella episode (*Purg.* II. 67–113) is a good passage for detailed analysis in these terms.

The literature of the medieval millennium has a unity not only of theme but also of characterization, especially female characterization. I stress the thread of influence that runs through the characterization of the female "wisdom figures" in many of these works, from Boethius' Lady Philosophy to Jean de Meun's Raison to Beatrice to the Pearl Maiden to Langland's Holy Church. This group of female figures with their biblical antecedents then provides a yardstick for comparison and contrast of other female characters such as Aude, Bramimonde, the Duenna, La Pia, Lady Bercilak.

Although this course is a period survey primarily for English majors, I spend a full half-semester on literature not written in England. There are theoretical and practical reasons for this design. I do not think I need argue strenuously that national and linguistic boundaries were not the significant dividing lines of culture in the medieval period, at least not in the literary sphere that I cover. It does not seem quite legitimate to me, for example, to study the *Pearl* without some reference to the *Purgatorio* or to the *Consolation of Philosophy.* Indeed, the pattern of influence running from what is now Italy to France and England in my course can be said to anticipate the pattern so characteristic of the Renaissance.

The practical considerations also bear noting. I teach few if any students preparing for graduate work in English, and those with such plans are usually aiming toward concentrations in later periods. Thus it does not behoove me to teach a very technical or specialized course on Middle English literature emphasizing language study and delving into the lesser works and writers. I want the students to come away with an appreciation of the great literature of a millennium, which they might otherwise never encounter. For the rare student who does need more depth in Middle English literature, I often schedule an extra tutorial hour each week and modify the assignment system.

Thus far, I have discussed course structure and linkage among works, but why teach only the *Purgatorio?* I prefer the *Purgatorio* to the other two canticles for various reasons. I view it as the most medieval of the three. The doctrine of spiritual purification after death as a preparation for the beatific vision was elaborated in the Middle Ages. Whereas hell is organized primarily according to an Aristotelian schema, the structure of purgatory proper follows the medieval pattern of the seven deadly sins. Whereas the concepts of hell and heaven are likely to be familiar to anyone brought up in the Western tradition, purgatory and the seven deadly sins are terra incognita even to some with Catholic backgrounds. Thus I have the fun of breaking new ground and of doing what I most like to do in the Walter Mitty side of my life, namely, teach theology. In addition, as a student of Charles Singleton, who in my opinion has done some of his best critical work on the *Purgatorio*, I relish the opportunity to share some of the insights about this canticle that I learned from him: the Exodus theme as the determinant of much imagery in the first nine cantos; the numerically symmetrical sequence of *Purgatorio* XIV–XX, which signals the theme central to the whole poem, the directionality of love and the crucial human vocation to make the right use of free will; the purgatorial process as a quest for personal justice, paradoxically at once superior and inferior to the original justice of prelapsarian Adam and Eve; and the "vistas in retrospect" that open up behind us only after we have reached certain nodal points in the poem.

I have another, perhaps idiosyncratic, reason. I think that the *Purgatorio* is for young adults, for people mature enough to have realized that choices have consequences and that we need to do battle with the nagging perversities at the core of ourselves, yet young enough for awareness that there is a way up. People in this frame of mind ought to be disposed to get beyond the dogmatic idiom and grasp the larger implications of the "moral" sense that Dante attributes, in the letter to Can Grande, to the Exodus theme and hence by association to the *Purgatorio:* "the turning of the soul from the sorrow and misery of sin to a state of grace." College students now are preoccupied with conversion and commitment, and by teaching the *Purgatorio*, I can introduce students to an authentic treatment of this theme, one with literary and intellectual grandeur and emotional finesse.

For methods, I rely heavily and unabashedly on lecturing. A good lecturer has to be enthusiastic, learned, organized, and purposeful. I have never had much luck at stimulating discussion in this particular course. I attribute this failure partly to my own clumsiness with the technique, partly to classes that are too big for discussion, and partly to the newness of the subject matter. The students and I know that I have much to tell them. And while I do use some slides early on to illustrate medieval iconography, and while I plan to preface the unit in the future with slides taken during a recent trip to Tuscany, I deliberately avoid such visual aids as maps and charts of purgatory in order to encourage students to get all the understanding they can from the poetry.

Because a long row of lectures can be boring, I have been experimenting during the past couple of years with ways of making students more active learners by trying to devise useful small-group exercises. The idea comes from *The Modern Practice of Adult Education* by Malcolm Knowles.[1] If certain caveats are observed, small-group exercises can be a refreshing and useful break in the pace of a class. First caveat: Small-group exercises cannot, as a rule, be made to happen spontaneously. If they are not to be mere time-wasters, they must be planned in advance and well integrated into the instructional schedule. Second caveat: The instructor should know clearly what he or she wishes the students to accomplish and must give precise directions. For example, the following might be directions for a lighthearted exercise near the start of the *Purgatorio* to see that students understand the point of the canticle and to suggest its relevance to contemporary concerns:

> Spend the next twenty-five minutes constructing a scheme for a modern purgatory. First, decide what are the basic tendencies to vice in our age, and then rank these in order of lessening importance. Be ready to defend your priorities. Choose one or more living persons to match with each of the tendencies you have identified, again justifying your choices and matchings. Choose a student to present your scheme to the class.

Third caveat: The task assigned should be specific, factual, and related to the students' primary need to master the text. For example, a request to classify Dante's characters according to a system worked out by the instructor and to draw conclusions from the results is apt to work pretty well. An attempt to get the students to find and discuss themes is apt to founder. Fourth caveat: The instructor should keep in mind that the main goals of these exercises are to get the students talking to one another about Dante and to promote *basic* learning: what happens, when, where, why, to whom.

Let me describe in detail the mechanics of what Knowles might call an "inquiry-group" exercise. I know before I start the course that by the time I am two-thirds through the unit on Dante, I will be lecturing breathlessly. The students might or might not be following me. Another hurried lecture will compound the problem, so before the semester begins, I plan a small-group review exercise for the fifth or sixth class of the Dante unit. Two classes ahead of time I announce the exercise, urging students to be caught up on the reading and reminding them that the work in groups is related to their class-participation grade. During the next class I hand out instructions suitable for the exercise as an incentive for advance preparation. On the day of the exercise I divide the students into groups or permit them to find their own; five per group is a workable limit, but duos and trios are fine too. Each group gets several cantos, and each appoints a spokesperson. The groups have an appropriate length of time to gather whatever information is requested. During the exercise I move from group to group to observe and to answer questions or to provoke the students to find their own answers. Each spokesperson then presents the findings of the group to the class. I find that with this procedure students question and correct one another, and overall student involvement is greater than in a plain discussion format. At the end of the exercise the students will have reviewed two-thirds of the poem, and I will have identified any glaring incomprehension. I can now move onward knowing that by and large the students are with me.

I hope it is evident from what I have said about the structure, themes, and philosophy of the course that I aim to emphasize the history of literature and of ideas, especially religious and psychological ideas. How effective is this approach? I have a tiger by the tail in addressing this vexing question of higher education research, how to measure "outcomes." I have never done a study designed to show whether my approach to teaching Dante results in more student learning and interest than some other approach might. Reading final examinations gives me the impression that students have learned something, sometimes a great deal. The real test is what the students think of the course—and whether they even remember it—five years afterward.

Present student reaction is clearly telling me not to change drastically what I am doing now in the classroom but to get better at doing it. I expect to keep teaching the *Purgatorio* much as I do now, though I hope with growing wisdom; and as I reflect on the relation between Vergil and Dante, ripening toward its termination, I also hope to learn from the poem more about my role as a teacher.

> . . . se' venuto in parte
> dov' io per me più oltre non discerno.
> Tratto t'ho qui con ingegno e con arte;
> lo tuo piacere omai prendi per duce.

. . . [you] are come to a part where I of myself discern no farther onward. I have brought you here with understanding and with art. Take henceforth your own pleasure for your guide.

(*Purg.* XXVII. 128–31)[2]

Notes

1 Malcolm Knowles, *The Modern Practice of Adult Education* (New York: Association Press, 1975). On pp. 289–90 Knowles outlines various "activity units" for learning different sorts of content. The four below seem to have the greatest potential for use in literature classes:

Topical discussion groups: groups organized for the purpose of reacting to, testing the meaning of, or sharing ideas about informational inputs from reading or speakers on given topics

Inquiry groups: groups organized to search out information and report their findings to the total assembly

Consultative groups: groups organized for the purpose of giving consultative help to one another

Learning-teaching teams: groups which take responsibility for learning all they can about a content unit and sharing what they have learned with the total assembly

2 Dante Alighieri, *The Divine Comedy: Purgatorio,* trans. Charles S. Singleton, Bollingen Series 80 (Princeton, N.J.: Princeton Univ. Press, 1973), II, Part 1, 298–99.

TEACHING DANTE IN AN INTERDISCIPLINARY CONTEXT

Theodora Graham

My first experiences teaching the *Inferno* were very different from my current course devoted to the Middle Ages. Trained in American and English literature, I was assigned to teach a world literature elective in an English department. I had not then visited Italy, and aside from alternately nostalgic or disquieting memories of youthful Catholicism, my familiarity with Dante's world was limited. Rereading the *Divine Comedy* reawakened my wonder and enthusiasm. I set about the usual scholarly survey of secondary sources, and armed with solid but predictable notes, diagrams, and questions, I resolved to make Dante relevant.

The objects of my zeal were a homogeneous group of nineteen-year-old sophomores attending a four-year college. Nearly all were English majors following a curriculum much like that of my own undergraduate days. The departmental book list for the course provided them and me with a comforting assurance; we studied the *Inferno* because like the other isolated "masterpieces" on the list, it was considered a sine qua non in the experience of a liberally educated college graduate. Our discussion of Dante completed, we moved confidently on to fourteenth-century England, sixteenth-century Spain, and nineteenth-century Russia, history catching up when it could.

While the classroom was often lively, a dimension seemed to be missing: we needed a better idea of the complexities of the world to which Dante responded in his work.

Then, in Wallace Stevens' words, "the theatre was changed / To something else." I now teach the *Divine Comedy* at an upper-division campus to a group of fifty junior-level students—graduates of different types of two-year institutions, retired military officers, veterans, homemakers, dropouts, ranging in age from nineteen to fifty-five. The course, Western Tradition II: Medieval and Renaissance Expressions in the Arts, is not a survey of literature appended to an English department but the second in a three-part series of interdisciplinary courses designed in 1967 as a core requirement in a program leading to a Bachelor of Humanities degree. Each four-credit course spans a ten-week term with four 75-minute periods a week. Other colleagues developed the sequence and its supporting philosophy before I arrived, but there have been no standard syllabi or texts. We have found that most students need a base, however, and each year we select one or more histories, such as F. Roy Willis' *Western Civilization: An Urban Perspective* and William Fleming's *Arts and Ideas.*[1]

Positing the view that Western concepts of self and the universe—fears, rituals, and values—may be understood through study of art forms, the Western Tradition series leads students to consider representative works of literature, visual art, music, and the allied arts as they interrelate within a cultural setting. These relations may be historical, with two works reflecting a social or political reality; thematic; archetypal; or formal, with two works of art in different media revealing a similar marriage of form and meaning.

In planning Western Tradition I, which includes the ancient Near East, Greece, and Rome, we assume that students have at best an uncertain sense of historical development and only limited experience, if any, in independent analysis of works of art. We survey students concerning their backgrounds (course work, travel, individual reading, music study, knowledge of the performing and plastic arts), but we assure them that a tabula rasa is not a disadvantage since they will be learning to think in new ways about the relation of the arts to culture. Furthermore, the instructors share the belief that the most effective learning procedures are in some degree inductive. Initial assignments and lectures, as well as study questions and other aids, assist students in formulating independent critical approaches and viewpoints, providing analytic strategies and expanding their critical vocabulary. The first course establishes a philosophical base and introduces ideas, traditions, and art forms that recur or influence subsequent concepts or works of art. Essentially, we ask this diverse group of students to create a frame of reference that approximates that of a knowledgeable participant in a culture different from their own but a culture historically relevant to the Western experience.

The *Divine Comedy* appears at midpoint in the second course, Medieval and Renaissance Expressions in the Arts. Students who follow the sequence in order begin this course with a knowledge of the classical world, a familiarity with representative Greco-Roman artifacts, and some skill in using a critical vocabulary.

Units prior to the *Divine Comedy* emphasize those aspects of the medieval period that found their culminating expressions in the writing of Dante and Chaucer: the architectural works at Ravenna, Cluny, and Chartres; the Gregorian chant and polyphonic motet; the philosophical system of Saint Thomas Aquinas; the paintings of Giotto; and for a sharp contrast, the Muslim artifacts of Córdoba and Granada. This is a tall order, for we must comprehend early Christianity, both Byzantine and Western, the expansion of Islam into the West, the continuing influence of the Greco-Roman world and medieval theologians' evolving attitudes toward Plato and Aristotle, the evolution of feudalism, chivalry and courtly love, and the conceptions of the universe, space, and position of human beings in it.

One means of acquiring an overview of these nine turbulent centuries is to use films. Two of Kenneth Clark's *Civilisation* series—*The Frozen World* and *The Great Thaw*—enable students to see landscape and setting, dimension and detail, which illustrations and slides merely suggest. Students soon become aware that Clark's personal view is impressionistic and occasionally reductive. Like Clark's commentary, John Canaday's in the short film *Chartres Cathedral* is also wanting in some respects. Yet the film's visual presentation is effective, showing the cathedral from multiple perspectives and following in schematic form architectural changes from the first Romanesque church to the Gothic sections. Another film that has a profound effect on many students is Ingmar Bergman's *The Seventh Seal.* Bergman's allegorical method affords comparisons with Dante's complex levels of allegory, and the threat of imminent death and everlasting punishment pervading the film make the plight of Dante's pilgrim and his torment more immediate.

Beginning then in the fourth century with early Christianity and the Neoplatonism that influenced its theology and art, the course first considers the contrasts between the political structures of the Eastern and Western empires and the clearly different church architecture each supported: Old St. Peter's, Sant' Apollinare (Classe), and Sant' Apollinare Nuovo (Ravenna), on the one hand; San Vitale (Ravenna) and the Hagia Sophia, on the other. That the basilica and central-type churches convey through their design a different attitude toward the worshiper is an idea reinforced in the iconography of their mosaics. Thus, early Christian symbolism introduces the students to the metaphysical equivalences they will encounter in all medieval art, at first obscure and puzzling to minds anchored to the literal and realistic.

Religious and sociopolitical aspects of feudalism are exemplified in our study of the *Song of Roland* and the Bayeux Tapestry. Slides of the Mosque of Córdoba indicate the powerful base the Muslims had established in Spain by the eighth century and help to clarify French hatred of the pagan intruders. The events of *Roland*, placed in the eighth century, encourage these connections, and its probable date of composition, the twelfth century, permits us to seek historical explanations for the reappearance of the epic form, as well as for construction on the grand scale in the cloister at Cluny and the churches of Saint Sernin at Toulouse and La Madeleine at Vézelay. Both the monastery of Cluny and Roland's story provide sources of imagery for the *Inferno*, and Ganelon, of course, finds his place with other traitors in Antenora. Students are pleased when they recognize the allusions themselves.

The predominantly masculine world of the chanson de geste, the Bayeux Tapestry, and the early monastic orders is shown to give way in part to the aristocratic ideals of courtly love and chivalry through our consideration of *Tristan and Iseult* and the much later, but extremely relevant, Unicorn Tapestries. A visiting music instructor's lecture on the troubadours and the Provençal lyric, highlighted by performance, makes Dante's extended use of these conventions of ritualized love in a religious context more comprehensible. The merging of secular and religious symbolism in the story of the unicorn hunt depicted on the tapestries evinces the apparent ease with which medieval men and women accepted such associations. Whether or not the veneration of the Virgin Mary influenced the idealization of the courtly lady, the beautiful and chaste—or faithful—woman did become, at least in literature, the means of inspiring and elevating the masculine imagination to accept self-denial and sacrifice and, ultimately, to achieve visions of Beauty and God.

The contrasts in values that underpin the stories of *Roland* and *Tristan*, the Bayeux and Unicorn tapestries, are fascinating to students. The evolution of church architecture in the West from the externally unadorned Sant' Apollinare to the richly sculptured facades of Chartres and Amiens, viewed in the light of changing attitudes toward representation of the human body and the function of sensuous beauty, is striking in even so brief an introduction. Entering Dante's world gradually, students are prepared to understand, if not to believe.

From close reading of the *Inferno*, guided by a single page of study questions, students draw ideas about the roles of major characters, allegorical levels of meaning, the merging of classical and Christian materials, stages of Dante's progress through hell, his use of the conventions of courtly love, and many of the sources of his imagery. Other handouts help to limit time given to background lectures: diagrams of the Ptolemaic universe, the major divisions of the three books, the progress of the journey through Easter week, for example. From Willis' *Western Civilization* students gain some idea of Florentine history prior to the Medicis. I suggest to those who are non-Catholics that they interview a practicing Catholic if editors' notes leave them puzzled about limbo, purgatory, the seven virtues and vices, confession, mortal and venial sins, and so forth, noting that modern Catholicism may not supply exact equivalents. For those who have not visited a European cathedral, I recommend a visit to an American cathedral nearby or to St. Patrick's in New York City or the National Cathedral in Washington, D.C.; and for contrast, a visit to the Ephrata Cloister (Ephrata, Pennsylvania), a Moravian church, or a large synagogue.

One of the most fruitful of the interrelations for understanding Dante is a comparison of Gothic architecture and the *Divine Comedy*. Limitation of space permits only a brief overview here, but the following points are very instructive to students. First, there is a direct analogy between the Gothic cathedral and the *Divine Comedy*: both are supremely ordered designs reflecting the divinely architected universe through mathematical symbolism and unity. Fleming's discussion of Chartres provides a helpful comparison of the trinitarian symbolism of the *Divine Comedy* with that of the Gothic cathedral (Fleming, pp. 154–60).

The encyclopedic character of medieval thought exemplified in both cathedral and poem is a second basis for comparison, as Henry Osborn Taylor has suggested: "if we cannot compare it [the *Divine Comedy*] with a *Summa*, we may certainly liken it to a cathedral, which also was a work of art and a *Summa salvationis* wrought in stone."[2] The sculpture and stained glass of Chartres, like Dante's discourses in the *Divine Comedy*, provide a complete summary of everything worth knowing, as well as models to esteem and imitate. A third comparison centers on the overwhelming presence of the Virgin Mary in both Gothic cathedrals and the *Divine Comedy*. The numerous works of art devoted to all aspects of the role of the Virgin Mary in Chartres, a cathedral dedicated to her, deepens students' understanding of

Dante's paeans to the Virgin and his description of the celestial rose. Finally, the same metaphysical conception of light that motivated Gothic builders to raise structures to unprecedented heights helps to explain the pervasive light imagery of the *Divine Comedy*. If the cathedral was to be an earthly reflection of the Heavenly City, bathed in the light of God, then illuminating the sanctuary with an ethereal light diffused by stained glass might intensify the worshiper's sense of the mystical presence of God. Likewise, Dante repeatedly associated the pilgrim's ascent to heaven with his accommodation to increasing intensities of light.

Dante's visual imagery in the *Inferno*, particularly his association of the bestial and grotesque with evil and torment, finds significant parallels in other works of medieval art, and these comparisons enrich discussion. Examples are available in illuminated manuscripts or Romanesque architectural sculpture: in capital decorations from the Abbey Church at Vézelay depicting an Angel Overcoming a Demon, or Lechery and Despair; in the Last Judgment tympanum of Autun Cathedral, whose grinning devils betray "the same nightmarish imagination . . . observed in the Romanesque animal world; they are composite creatures, human in general outline but with spidery, bird-like legs, furry thighs, tails, pointed ears, and enormous mouths."[3] That Christians of this earlier period conceived of hell in vivid, concrete terms is clear from these relief figures. In Giotto's fresco of the *Last Judgment* in the Arena Chapel and Maitani's *Last Judgment* on the facade of Orvieto Cathedral appear other representations of the torments of the damned that Dante's contemporaries would have known. In Dante's hell, aside from the three beasts of Canto I, demonic figures are usually drawn from Greek mythology. But men, too, may be reduced to animals: Filippo Argenti and Bocca are "curs"; Vanni Fucci, a "beast" for whom Pistoia was a "fitting den." In Canto XXVI Florence in her pride is compared to a great bird with outstretched wings, a description, Mark Musa observes, that prefigures the poet's image of Lucifer.

There is little doubt that introducing even a few of these interrelations in our study of the *Divine Comedy* requires time, and some might argue that time would be better given to a close consideration of the poem itself. I believe, however, that a person who genuinely discovers Dante's work the first time will go on to read it again and that even a person who is neither by temperament nor by education a lover of literature will derive understanding and pleasure from this approach; furthermore, both persons will share valuable insights into a world very different from our own. That the text, painting, or building must be primary in our approach is a principle worth restating. We study works of visual art and music to assess their artistic values, not merely to reinforce literary ideas. Giotto's frescoes of the *Stigmatization of Saint Francis* and *Saint Francis Renouncing His Worldly Goods* in the Bardi Chapel of the Church of Santa Croce are important to us as works of art, and not simply because they reveal an original treatment of subject and interest in psychology that help us to define Dante's greatness. Selection is the most difficult part of our task: what do we leave out? what do we sacrifice? Answering this question makes each annual encounter with the *Divine Comedy* new and vital.

Notes

[1] F. Roy Willis, *Western Civilization: An Urban Perspective*, 3rd ed. (Boston: Heath, 1981); William Fleming, *Arts and Ideas*, 6th ed. (New York: Holt, 1980).

[2] Henry Osborn Taylor, *The Mediaeval Mind*, 4th ed. (Cambridge, Mass.: Harvard Univ. Press, 1966), II, 569.

[3] H. W. Janson, *History of Art*, rev. ed. (Englewood Cliffs, N.J.: Prentice-Hall, 1969), p. 222. See also Barbara Nolan's comparison of the Autun and St. Denis tympana in *The Gothic Visionary Perspective* (Princeton: Princeton Univ. Press, 1977), pp. 45–47.

DANTE: GATEWAY TO THE HUMANITIES

John B. Harcourt

The seminar is for freshmen and includes students from the liberal arts and various professional curricula. The text is the complete *Divine Comedy* (in John Ciardi's translation). The title of the course is Dante: Gateway to the Humanities.

Surely this combination is an invitation to trouble, and the protests begin to surface within the first few meetings. How could anyone, even back then in the "Dark" Ages, actually believe in hell, God's private torture chamber? Punishment without end? without purpose? without hope of rehabilitation and eventual forgiveness? Surely human sensibilities are revolted by such a spectacle, and a poet who revels in detailing its horrors can only be described as sick, and the poem a sadistic obscenity.

The inscription over the gate of hell serves to focus the uproar: "SACRED JUSTICE MOVED MY ARCHITECT. / I WAS RAISED HERE BY DI-VINE OMNIPOTENCE, / PRIMORDIAL LOVE AND ULTIMATE INTEL-LECT."[1] Omnipotence? The students grudgingly allow that God (as-suming his existence) *could* have made a hell if he had so desired and if his "ultimate intellect" had foreseen a need for it. Sacred justice? Only on some primitive, vengeful level, unworthy of civilized human beings, to say nothing of a deity. But "primordial love"? Surely Dante had to be kidding.

At this point I find it strategic to back away from the medieval text and to turn to Jean-Paul Sartre's *No Exit*. There are distinct advantages in being able to point out that a twentieth-century atheistic existentialist has devoted a play to damnation as a metaphor of our human condition. Consideration of Sartre's reasons for resurrecting this unlikely item from the scrap heap of religion may help in explaining Dante. Thus, shamelessly exploiting the current mystique of existentialism, I set forth a few hypotheses that the seminar will test:

1. Reading Dante requires no belief in the traditional Judeo-Christian God, in life after death, or in a system of cosmic rewards and punishments.
2. What is required is a belief in men and women as intensely concerned with their universe, their mortality, their fate; as free to choose, although admittedly among limited options; as able in some mysterious fashion to "make themselves" through their free decisions, each new decision subsuming all the previous decisions, the final decision of an individual's life then becoming the truth about that man or woman, a truth so absolute that not even divine fiat can alter it.
3. To be liberally educated, a person must cultivate an attitude of openness toward reality based on the certainty that no model, whether religious, philosophical, or scientific, is more than a faint, far-off reflection of an unknowable mystery, merely the shadows flickering on the wall of Plato's cave.

Garcin, Estelle, and Inez, the characters of *No Exit*, provide a readily accessible demonstration of the implications of an existential affirmation of our radical freedom and of the processes by which we create our own essence up to the moment of final truth. Intimations of the *mysterium tremendum* will come more slowly.

Students can be induced to accept, at least provisionally, the concept of our freedom of choice, but they remain bothered by both Sartre's and Dante's insistence on the significance of the last minutes of a person's life. Is it fair, I am asked, to condemn a man who for sixty or seventy years has led a useful, good life but who, in the terminal moments of hospitalized consciousness, lusts after his nurse? The innate sentimentality of American educational institutions creates a marked preference for striking a four-year cumulative average rather than, say, risking all on a comprehensive examination at the end of the senior year. Yet even freshmen can be persuaded that ideally a degree should certify to society what a person *has become* and *is* at the time it is conferred. Those unruly impulses of the dying man just might express the submerged reality that had been suppressed throughout a lifetime of dull unauthentic conformity.

Now the imaginative vividness of Dante's key images comes to our rescue. Invoking (without naming it) the principle of *contrapasso*, one can readily demonstrate that the punishment is not really a punishment at all, not a sentence imposed by an external judge, but rather a revelation of the inner truth of a human life, a public disclosure, as it were, of what that person was really like inside by the end of the lifelong process of self-creation. Every canto of the *Inferno* displays Dante's profound intuition of what a particular kind of evil *feels like* in the most literal sense, in that devastating clarity of the morning after, when all the self-exculpating rationalizations have been stripped away. The *Purgatorio* is likewise inexhaustibly rich in studies of moral kinesthesia. I ask members of the seminar to feel proud, to induce, then and there, a sense of arrogant superiority to every other member of the group, to become aware of the slight, involuntary thrusting back of the shoulders, the elevation of the head, and then to view the punishment of the proud on the first terrace in the light of that experience. Or to look at some member of the class with envy, to feel the eye muscles contracting to a malevolent squint, and then to consider the sewn-up eyes of the envious. Or to savor the implications of "I was so mad I couldn't see straight" in relation to the acrid smoke on the terrace of the angry. An entire semester could easily be devoted just to explicating the psychological profundity and the physiological accuracy of Dante's ethical categories.

Perhaps at this point all of this can be accepted as a possible view of the intrinsic, self-administering laws of justice. Maybe the wages of sin do come COD, as one of my professors once observed. But Dante goes much further than the impersonal, self-righting mechanism delineated in Ralph Waldo Emerson's essay "Compensation." What *are* we to make of his insistence that "primordial love" is somehow involved in hell? Fortunately, no one is more aware than the middle-class American college student that love requires a certain amount of elbowroom, that love, particularly parental love, requires an acceptance of the beloved's independent reality, of his or her decisions even when, especially when, we are most appalled by those decisions and their consequences. Dante therefore invites us to consider the possibility that our highest human perceptions of love may point toward the dimensions of Love absolutely conceived, that whatever power confers on us our mysterious freedom must respect the use of that freedom, which, if in fact it is freedom, must imply the ability not only to choose evil but also to choose it definitively, irrevocably. The God of the *Commedia*, the Love that created hell, may thus point to the ultimate measure, the ultimate anguish, of all loving, the willingness to accept the reality of final rejection, precisely out of continuing and indestructible love for the freedom of the beloved. Despite their recriminations, the citizens of Dante's hell have been granted what they wanted most of all: the right to be wrong on their own terms, forever.

So far we have sidestepped the question of the meaning of good and evil, but at some point early in the semester we must address it squarely. Granted the possibility of freedom, what does it mean to choose good or evil? Discussion almost immediately breaks down here into a defeated relativism of the "I'm OK, you're OK" variety. Occasionally someone remembers Hemingway's dictum: "What is moral is what you feel good after and what is immoral is what you feel bad after." In contrast to such simplicities, Dante's incredibly convoluted moral universe must at first seem a monumental exercise in misplaced ingenuity. How can actions be objectively categorized? How can they be ordered in so hierarchical a structure that even the most casual reader soon learns that whenever Dante scrambles down a cliffside or finds a stair cut in purgatorial rock or orbits with the speed of light from sphere to paradisal sphere, we are invited to attend to a descent into greater evil or to a climbing toward ultimate good? Even whatever rudimentary moral ranking our culture permits is outraged by what the text reveals. Why are the adulterers in the second circle and the gluttons below them in the third? Can Dante be saying that sitting in the snack bar shoveling down banana splits is more reprehensible than sexual hanky-panky?

Hemingway's facile witticism can serve at least as a starting point. Why do we feel "good" after action A but "bad" after action B? Long silences, many false starts, much embarrassment all around. Eventually, someone resorts to the clichés about self-fulfillment and self-realization. But what fulfills us? How do we realize ourselves? Sooner or later we achieve some measure of consensus that whatever builds up life is good, and whatever erodes or destroys it is evil. And as the concept of an integrated personality begins to emerge (with some assistance from popular psychology and sociology), the insight dawns that affirming life has something to do with our capacity to love, while its opposite involves deflecting and twisting love into the myriad forms of hatefulness. From then on, Dante's system needs only careful and patient explication. Those adulterers were at least relating to their fellow human beings; the gluttons had fixated on something subhuman (though food is potentially a sacrament of fellowship and life, so that the condition of the miser, still farther down, is even worse, his clutch having closed only on dead things in anxiety-ridden secrecy). The awareness of moral hierarchy can be sharpened by asking students to place in the circles of hell some ostensibly new categories of wrongdoing: racism, pollution of the environment, pushing drugs.

The ethical classifications, the rewards and punishments, can thus be interpreted existentially and humanistically. In fact, Dante's pilgrimage is curiously amenable to psychoanalytical analogies, especially in its metaphors of spatiality and direction. The journey through hell is a descent into the depths of human personality, from the less serious distortions of our capacity to love down, in a meticulously graduated progression, to that ultimate horror of our inner landscape, the image of absolute self-centeredness sealed off forever from every human contact in a lake of ice. After confronting the full extent of our sickness, Dante is reoriented and emerges to begin the rehabilitative therapy up the slopes of Mount Purgatory. There, the order is reversed. As in medical practice, the most serious problems are dealt with first; then all the lesser disturbances fall away one by one. And as Vergil slips away, Dante, cured, realizes that he no longer needs his therapist.

Each year I am tempted to stop there, at the end of the second canticle. Diagnosis and cure, analysis and therapy are easy to accommodate to the range of contemporary thought; our limitation to the City of Man lends a certain appeal to stopping at the Earthly Paradise.

Paradoxically, I have found that the way to the Empyrean lies through a heavy emphasis on Dante's this-worldliness. The students find it too easy to fall back on stereotypes: Dante was "medieval" and therefore "otherworldly." It is a bit of a shock when they discover that this "otherworldly" Dante, committed though he may have been to the Ptolemaic world picture, nevertheless leaves us far behind in his ability to detail the phenomena of the physical universe. Not a single student can ever identify the phase of the moon on the previous night, to say nothing of explaining the precession of the equinoxes, or the sun's apparent journey back along the zodiacal constellations and its spiraling annual course between the boundaries of the tropics. And what can we make of Dante's passionate involvement with the fourteenth-century political scene, not only in Florence but throughout the known world? Most of us flunk the simplest of impromptu questionnaires on contemporary national or international events and personages. Dante, like Chaucer, is an affront to our sense of smug evolutionary superiority, as gradually the realization dawns that in many important respects, medieval people were more aware, more intellectually agile, more imaginative—in a word, more sophisticated—than we are.

Once Dante has won the students' respect as meticulous observer of, and passionately committed actor in, the sublunary scene, there is a basis for assessing his more audacious claims. For Dante, space and time, matter and history, were sacramental: they pointed toward a pervasive and ultimately triumphant purposefulness deep in the heart of things. His reality was nothing less than a "tri-Unity," whose proper name was Love—the only source, the only goal, of all our human longing. Now the tactical problem is to help students overcome a deep-seated suspicion of beatitude.

Semantic transpositions help a little. I resort to capitalized abstractions like Reality or Being (even Ultimate Reality or Total Being) in lieu of an all too anthropomorphic image of God precipitated by the religiosity of Sunday school and sermon. And without frightening anyone by using its proper name, I invoke the principle of ontological analogy: if we are alive, if we are free, if we are conscious and capable of love, then those values may not be totally alien to the universe that somehow has managed to produce both us and them. I offhandedly mention that a quite respectable twentieth-century scientist, Teilhard de Chardin, has set forth an integrated vision of reality from Big Bang to Omega Point that, in sheer scope and drama, invites comparison with Dante's cosmos. One or two will go out looking for *The Phenomenon of Man*.

But I gain the most, I think, simply by setting the *Paradiso* side by side with a near-contemporary utopian blueprint, the nineteenth-century novel *Looking Backward* by Edward Bellamy. I contrast Bellamy's tidy, efficient, gracious Boston of the year 2000, its harmoniously integrated personalities, its useful men and women, and its ingenious reconciliation of freedom and a rational distribution of the world's goods, with the ecstasies of beatitude so compellingly articulated in Dante's final cantos. To pit the magic of supreme poetry against the sober decencies of a psychology of adjustment and a sociology of universal welfare is certainly not wholly fair, but it makes its point effectively. Finally, I read the Italian of *Paradiso* XXXIII aloud, letting its dazzling succession of images, its unearthly harmonies, wash over us, and the power of the medieval poem, as a poem, comes through triumphantly.

Dante, then, may be allowed, at least provisionally, his glimpse of the Love that moves the sun and other stars. But, the students ask, can it be more than a glimpse, a glimpse available only at certain moments and to certain kinds of people? What perplexes them is Dante's conviction that his totally ordered vision, with its sweep of interlocking entities ranging from the infinity of God to the very verge of nonbeing, is accessible not just to mystics but to everyman, to any intellect that opens itself to the promptings of divine grace.

To point up this outrageous claim, I turn to *The Waste Land*. From the vantage of T. S. Eliot's poem, we look back over the totality of the Western cultural tradition, the figures Dante knew and all the others whom he could not have known. This tradition the fourteenth-century poet could exuberantly exploit. But by 1922, Vergil and Ovid, the Bible, Dante himself (along with Shakespeare, Spenser, and Milton) could seem only the withered stumps of time, a heap of broken images, the fragments that the later poet can only clutch to shore against his ruins. Dante's linked tercets, his architectonic parallelisms, his unifying vision—these we review against the discontinuities, the discordant voices, the blurred intimations of a wholly tentative significance offered by the modern poem. Happily, since we are now a post–*Waste Land* generation, since Eliot's poem has itself become yet another monument in our cultural history, we can then consider whether his epitaph for Western civilization may have been premature, whether Dante may not offer hope that some future century may also write its *Divine Comedy*. The Italian poet's vision of order (I suggest, but do not insist) may yet be found to be an essential dimension of our humanity.

The students can only begin to respond on these levels, of course. The *Divine Comedy* is a kind of educational time bomb that may detonate at some unforeseen moment beyond the freshman seminar, beyond the college years. More immediately, "nel mezzo del cammin" of our semester, the time comes for the strictly practical matter of preregistration for the following term. Together we formulate some of the key human questions that have emerged in our dialogues. Once these have been articulated, I urge students to carry them to their academic advisers with the demand that a series of courses be arranged that will point toward possible answers. This process, once begun, is self-fueling and far more likely than any "core curriculum" to energize a truly liberating and humanizing education. And if the experience of the past repeats itself, a few of the students will return to me in their senior year and ask, "Can we talk a little more about Dante? I think I'm just beginning to see what the guy was driving at."

Note

[1] All Dante quotations in English are from John Ciardi, trans., *The Divine Comedy* (New York: Norton, 1970).

THE *DIVINE COMEDY* AS A MAP OF THE WAY TO HAPPINESS

Sister Mary Clemente Davlin, O.P.

For an American undergraduate, a first reading of the *Divine Comedy* seems surrounded with difficulties. The complexity of a long text written in an unfamiliar symbolic allegorical form is increased by our distance from the year 1321 and our consequent unfamiliarity with many characters, places, symbols, and ideas that Dante's first readers took for granted. The vast number of commentaries on the poem, and even the length and detail of notes and diagrams in the best text editions and study guides, tend to overwhelm a student, and although translations are easily available for those unfamiliar with Italian, none has the attractiveness of the original. Moreover, most students have encountered repellent stereotypes of Dante as a vindictive fanatic, and many are puzzled about how to understand and feel at home in a poem so apparently alien, whose very richness of meaning may be bewildering.

Yet in spite of all these difficulties, the *Divine Comedy* is one of the most exciting and rewarding of all texts to study or to teach, whether in a full semester course or as a unit in World Literature. The course I describe here, Dante in Translation, is a semester course for four credits, built on insights and principles learned from my teachers, Emma Detti of Florence and Enrico De' Negri of Pisa and Berkeley; my friend, the late Ruth Mary Fox of Wisconsin; and my students.

136

The aims of such a course in the *Divine Comedy*, I believe, are simply the reading, understanding, and enjoyment of the poem, but their achievement depends on overcoming the difficulties I have mentioned. It is necessary first for students to want to read the *Divine Comedy*, in Italian if possible, and therefore to know something about Dante and about what the experience of reading the *Divine Comedy* can offer them. They need to know a little about the period and presuppositions of the author. And they need the encouragement of a simple method of reading the poem, so that they will not be put off by the multiplicity and detail of notes and commentaries but rather use them with profit.

One or two introductory classes suffice to introduce Dante in a historical context, and they should serve to increase the students' desire to read the poem. A discussion of Michele Barbi's *Life of Dante* shows Dante to be an extraordinary person: lover, student, soldier, statesman, family man, patriot, teacher, visionary, and poet. If the teacher prepares a chronological table setting the events of Dante's life beside contemporary history, students will see, for example, that in Dante's early childhood, Roger Bacon worked, Giotto was born, and Saint Louis of France died; Aquinas and Bonaventure died the year Dante first saw Beatrice; Petrarch and Boccaccio were born, the Arena Chapel frescoes were painted, and Duns Scotus died during the torturing years of Dante's exile. With the help of such facts, some pictures, and some discussion, students will begin to put together information from other reading and courses and to see Dante as part of a vital, creative period that they have the chance to experience from the inside by reading the *Divine Comedy*.

In order to reduce multiple facts to a comprehensible order and to show the medieval genius as an accessible person, I first present Dante as a man with two great loves: the love for a woman and the love for a city. Selections from the *Vita nuova* tell students the story of Dante's transforming love for Beatrice in his own words, ending with his promise "to write of her that which has never been written of any other woman." Because he kept that promise in the *Divine Comedy*, students can approach it as a supreme love poem and a poem of discovery that shows for the first time in our literature how the deep human love of a man and woman for one another can lead to "the Love that moves the sun and the other stars." Thus, reading the *Divine Comedy* is a way to learn love.

It is harder for modern Americans who have grown up in a mobile society to comprehend Dante's love for the city of Florence. Yet only his passionate love for this free city can explain many experiences of his life: the tragedy of having to condemn his friend Guido Cavalcanti to an exile that ended in death; the intensity of Dante's struggles as an ambassador to keep papal and French forces from overrunning Florence; the bitterness of being betrayed in that struggle; the anguish of a perpetual exile that he has his ancestor describe in the *Paradiso:* "You shall leave behind each most dearly beloved thing . . . you will find out how salt the bread of other people tastes, how hard it is to climb another's stairs." (*Par.* XVII. 55–56, 58–60; translations throughout are mine). Only this love explains his invectives against the corruption of Florence that rage through the *Divine Comedy* and his poignant desire to return and be crowned with laurel there. Finally, this love explains why Farinata of *Inferno* X, enemy to Dante's party and dead before Dante's birth, is yet such a hero to the poet. It was Farinata "alone, there where everyone agreed to destroy Florence, who openly defended her" (*Inf.* X. 91–93), and Dante, like Farinata, would refuse in 1304 to participate in a war aimed at the destruction of his city. So the *Divine Comedy* may be read not only as a love poem but also as a political poem—a poem about history and freedom and about a city that still lives. Students who have visited Florence can bring slides of the city to class; any good guidebook to Florence will help the teacher to point out which civic buildings and Florentine art works Dante knew. Seeing Dante's city helps students understand his poem; his image of angels, for example, has no relation to the pink and blue cherubs we see in popular pious art today but derives from awesome Byzantine figures in the Baptistery mosaics. With the aid of a guide sheet, some slides, some travel stories, and a few books on reserve, all students can grasp something of the beauty and spirit of Florence.

One of Dante's other loves also needs to be understood: his love for the Church as the people of God, the bride of Christ. Dante presupposed a clear distinction between temporal and spiritual authority, and in religious matters, a distinction between interior reality and exterior sign. He loved and believed in the Church, and therefore, like Peter in *Paradiso* XXVII, he attacked and despised all that lessened her holiness.

When students in a course of this kind come from many majors, it is especially helpful for them to realize that the *Divine Comedy* is a whole world, and that not only love, politics, and religion but whatever they are interested in can be found there. Ruth Mary Fox used to encourage her students to search out in the text Dante's physics of light, his understanding of astronomy and cosmology and of love and friendship, as well as the history of Italy, music, angelology, linguistics, geography, psychology, ethics, philosophy, and theologies.

But how should one read the *Divine Comedy?* For it is more than autobiography, invective, and encyclopedia. My own experience has been that while students need to become aware that the poem may be read on at least four levels, they will find two of these levels easiest and most rewarding to explore on a first reading—literal narrative and psychological allegory. The poem can be read and perhaps should first be read literally, as fantasy: the science-fiction adventure of a traveler among ghosts, monsters, and angels, and on interplanetary flight. This literal reading is easy and gripping, demands little help from a teacher, and overturns many negative presuppositions about the poem. But it leaves most of the poem's symbolism untapped and most readers unsatisfied. A course in Dante, I believe, can most successfully emphasize a second kind of interpretation, a psychological reading.

The psychological reading on which this course is based derives from Dorothy Sayers' studies of the *sensus moralis*.[1] This is a reading of the *Divine Comedy* as Dante's exploration of the human heart and human society in this world. The *Inferno* is not only hell: it is also human life when life has become a hell. It is the closed human heart, a funnel of dissipation, violence, and malice; it is personal and communal evil experienced as a dark, chilling descent.

Everyone knows that life can be such a hell, and Dante shows why. One thinks of Lear's words: "Then let them anatomize Regan. See what breeds about her heart. Is there any cause in nature that makes these hard hearts?" (*King Lear* III.vi.77–79). Dante's *Inferno* is such an anatomy. The *contrapasso* of each circle thus can be read not so much as a punishment for sin but rather as the true nature of sin itself. What are murder and tyranny but choosing to be steeped in the blood of others in order to achieve one's aims? What is betrayal but turning one's heart to ice so that no natural warmth remains? In the notes to her translation, Sayers suggests a method but leaves it to the reader to work out details and implications of this reading. As students work them out, they learn to read an allegory, and Dante's hell gradually reveals itself not as a bizarre book of horrible arbitrary punishments in another world but as a clinically accurate unmasking of human corruption in this world. Corruption, for Dante, is always a matter of choice, for sin is hell, and one can sin only by choice. The horror is that no characters in hell express a wish to get out; they are held there by their own continuing choice. As Sayers points out, Dante explores not only the individual human heart, but also the human community, "the city." What does the blind pursuit of desire make of a society? What does the choice to live by violence do to a nation? What becomes of a people who live by fraud and malice? The three parts of hell are Dante's answer, so detailed and complex that after six hundred years, readers can still find new, healing insights there.

Many people believe that the *Inferno* is the finest part of the *Divine Comedy* and hence leave the *Purgatorio* and the *Paradiso* undiscovered. But the *Purgatorio* is the most practical and challenging canticle, mapping the climb toward happiness and freedom, the slow, possible journey toward true humanness, true love, which is the purpose of life in this world. Each terrace is a complete program for growth in a particular aspect of love. Those with ungoverned tempers who live with their heads in the smoke of irascibility need to reach out and cling to others, trying to walk in harmony with them, meditating on the folly of wrath and the wisdom of gentleness, and praying, "Lamb of God, grant us peace." The proud can become loving by bending to walk with others on the human level of earth, learning to pray, "Thy will be done." Enrico De' Negri has shown that within this patterned program each character in the *Purgatorio* illustrates a unique step in the healing process.[2] The purgatory is really a map of how to become holy, happy, and whole, perhaps the most detailed and humanly understandable map ever made. No theological text, I believe, so clearly distinguishes human temptation from deliberate sin as Dante's dream of the "femmina balba" (*Purg.* XIX); no one since Augustine so vividly shows that only love can save from lust (*Purg.* XXVII), that we must, in Eliot's paraphrase, "be redeemed from fire by fire" ("Little Gidding" IV.8).

And what is left for heaven? As Shelley observed in *A Defence of Poetry*, the *Paradiso* is "the most glorious imagination of modern poetry . . . a perpetual hymn of everlasting love." This mysterious canticle is the way life could be, the way life can gradually become, for it shows how people of every kind act if their love is perfect. Teachers become suns, torches, jewels; they dance, and bring brilliant, joyful light to others (*Par.* X–XIII). Those who endure suffering with courage and integrity are not simply heroes; mystically they become the crucified, redeeming Christ for others (*Par.* XIV). All who love become more and more themselves yet mysteriously united in beauty and vitality for those who have eyes to see; they become like petals of a rose, which is the city of God. In this reading, paradise is not only the eternal reward but also human life here and now if it is lived in love.

Such an allegorical reading of the *Divine Comedy* is, of course, only one of many possible ways to read it. It proves a tantalizing, compelling one to modern students, and most assignments and exercises in this course are designed to enable students to read in this way.

In a three- or four-semester-hour course in the *Divine Comedy* in translation, students can study about five cantos for each class meeting, using Sinclair's text so that those who know even a little Italian can read some or all in the original. Sayers' notes and charts, Grandgent's notes, and Singleton's commentaries should be available on a reserve shelf, so that students can come to understand each word of the text. In most class periods, the teacher can answer questions, comment on style, characterization, structure and development of narrative, and suggest things to look for in the next few cantos. Occasionally, a discussion should be held on a broad question, enabling students to grasp with increasing security the allegorical method of reading. For example, after reading Cantos I to VIII on upper hell, they might discuss the relevance to Dante of Dostoevsky's words, "What is hell? I maintain that it is the inability to love."

Besides studying and discussing the text and doing some critical reading (I assign essays in Irma Brandeis' *Discussions of the* Divine Comedy), seven exercises help students to organize the detail of the *Divine Comedy* and perceive meaning in it. Three of these are simple one-page charts of the three canticles, made while reading; it is valuable to have one's own chart, not simply a published one, for help in visualizing structures and remembering characters. After reading all of the *Inferno*, two other exercises are helpful. One is the making of a hell by each student or group of students. They choose from one to three circles of Dante's hell and people them with historical or contemporary figures, groups, or actions of their own choice (not, of course, suggesting that these people are actually in hell but using them as Dante used his characters, symbolically.) Some students tear photos, stories, or ads from newspapers or magazines, using, for example, pictures of mob violence, Ku Klux Klan activities, arson, war, and riots to illustrate the seventh circle in a dramatic contemporary way; others draw or dramatize a part of hell. In their presentations, students help one another see the selective symbolic nature of Dante's characters and an allegorical meaning of his hell.

Another exercise is a short paper (two or three pages) tracing one symbol through one episode in hell and analyzing its meanings, trying to see some of the things the symbol suggests about life if hell is life or life is hell. A similar exercise may be done after reading the *Purgatorio:* if Dante's purgatory is a way of becoming happier and more whole in this life, what does this short section prescribe, and how? To write such a paper means translating symbol into meaning, deciphering posture and color, action and setting; the insights gained are sometimes profound. The last exercise is a short research paper on a sharply limited subject, designed to be suitable for entry in the annual competition of the Dante Society of America or for submission as a paper at a scholarly meeting. Brevity and the possibility of competition help motivate better students to do original scholarly papers.

Two field trips are useful supplements in helping students understand purgatory and paradise. As Enrico De' Negri has pointed out, the *Purgatorio* is a penitential poem, built on Dante's profound understanding of sin and the sacrament of penance or reconciliation.[3] Its symbolism will make more sense to modern students if they can observe a Roman Catholic reconciliation service and/or an Ash Wednesday service. The liturgical ceremonies are remarkably relevant to the *Divine Comedy*, for they make similar symbolic use of color, water, bodily posture, and clothing. On Ash Wednesday, for example, at the threshold of Lent, the priest marks the penitent's forehead as the angel marks Dante's at the threshold of purgatory (*Purg.* IX). The reconciliation service and the poem express the same understanding of sin as a wound, of reconciliation as a process within the body of believers, and of penance as prayerful activity designed to further healing. Other symbolism in purgatory is liturgical, too, of course, and attendance at a Corpus Christi procession will help to clarify *Purgatorio* XXX, a public baptism or an Easter Vigil service will clarify *Purgatorio* XXXI, and a compline procession in a large monastery or convent will clarify *Purgatorio* VIII. Inviting a colleague from the music department to sing Dante's songs and prayers to the class and to explain their place in the liturgical year and day is another source of understanding.

A trip to a planetarium is valuable when the class is reading the *Paradiso*. Even if a historian of science is not available to explain differences between the Ptolemaic and Copernican systems, a good modern film or presentation on the planets and their orbits provides knowledge of Dante's contextual structure, stimulates students visually to appreciate the poetry of the *Paradiso*, and shows how vitally poetry and science were linked in Dante's mind.

If a whole course in the *Divine Comedy* is not possible, then a good introduction may be made in a five-week unit, using the same methods, assigning the *Inferno* but allowing students to skim cantos XVIII–XXV, assigning the whole *Purgatorio*, and assigning at least Cantos I–III, X–XII, XXIV–XXVI, XXX–XXXIII of the *Paradiso*.

The crucial thing in this first reading of Dante is not memorization of detail, though that has a place, but understanding and delight. At the end of the course or unit, students should have made the journey, should know characters and understand relations; they should see the structures that shape the poem; they should understand the sense of evil, of love, and of human conversion and growth that informs the

Divine Comedy. Understanding all this, they will have found delight as, "eager to listen," they "follow after [Dante's] singing ship" (*Par.* II. 1–3).

Notes

¹ Dorothy Sayers, Introd., *Hell,* Vol. I of *The Comedy of Dante Alighieri* (Baltimore: Penguin, 1949), pp. 17, 19, 68.

² Unpublished lectures at the University of California, Berkeley. See De' Negri, "Tema e iconografia del Purgatorio," *Romanic Review,* 49 (1958), 86 and passim.

³ Unpublished paper delivered at Dante Symposium, Edgewood College, 16 October, 1965. See also his "L'inferno di Dante e la teologia penitenziale," *Annali della Scuola Normale Superiore di Pisa,* 4 (1974), 189–223.

COURSE SYLLABUS

WEEK

1   Introduction to course.
Dante's two loves. Read Barbi's *Life of Dante* and be prepared to discuss it. If you have slides of Florence you would like to share, bring and explain them in relation to Dante's life.

Part I: The Closed Heart

2   *Inf.* I–II: the dark forest. How to read the poem: image, symbol, allegory.
Inf. III–VIII. 66: upper hell (incontinence). Begin your chart. Write down and bring to class two questions you would like answered or discussed in the next class.
Small discussion groups. Discussion of your questions and of Dostoevsky's question, "What is hell?"

3   *Inf.* VIII. 67–XI: the city of Dis, a crisis, and circle six (turning from the truth).
Ash Wednesday. *Inf.* XII–XVI: the violent. Try to observe carefully a Catholic ceremony of ashes today and a ceremony of reconciliation (penance service) when you can. Write down your observations of materials used, postures, words, symbolism, spirit. It will help you understand the *Purgatorio* and to discover why Dante descended into hell during Lent.
Inf. XVII–XXII: Malebolge, fraud; the first four trenches and another crisis.

4   *Inf.* XXIII–XXX: Malebolge, the last six trenches.
Inf. XXXI–XXXIV: the cold heart of hell.
Bring your chart of hell. As you read and reread the *Inferno*, make a simple one-page chart of hell to help you see its structure. You may want to look at published charts, such as Sinclair's or Sayers', but make yours personal and useful. Lecture-demonstration: famous illustrations of Dante's hell.

5   Quiz on hell.
Paper due. Write a brief paper (2 or 3 pages typed) tracing one symbol through one episode in hell and analyzing its meanings. Choose, for example, a color, a sound, light, sand, heat, fire, bodily posture, physical motion, etc. Underline every use of it in your episode. Try to see patterns in its use; try to see some of the things your symbol suggests about life, if hell is life.

Small-group discussions: "What is hell?" "What is sin?" Exercise due. Create a hell of your own. Choose from one to three circles of Dante's hell, and put people, historical or contemporary figures or groups, into them. You might want to use a single day's newspaper for material or to range over history. Bring the exercise to share and discuss.

Part II: Climbing the Seven Story Mountain

6   Introduction to purgatory: read Cantos XVII–XVIII.
    Purg. I–V: the beach (antepurgatory).
    Purg. VI–IX: the beach, the first garden, and the gate.
    Visual structure of the *Purgatorio:* what to look for.

7   *Purg.* X–XIV: the first and second stories: learning humility and generosity. Begin your chart.
    Purg. XV–XIX: the third and fourth stories: learning peace and zeal.
    Field trip: medieval art in the Art Institute of Chicago. Skim Auerbach, "Figural Art in the *Divine Comedy*," Wicksteed, "Hell," and Fergusson, "Metaphor of the Journey" in *Discussions of the Divine Comedy*, edited by Irma Brandeis. Write down your questions. You may want to prepare for the field trip by reading about medieval art, architecture, or crafts in reference or history books.

8   *Purg.* XX–XXV. 108: the fifth and sixth stories: learning mastery over money, food, and drink.
    Purg. XXV. 109–XXVIII the last story: from lust to love, the sacred garden, the Earthly Paradise. Skim Ruskin's "Dante's Landscape" in Brandeis.

9   *Purg.* XXIX–XXXIII: the pageant in the Earthly Paradise, the meeting with Beatrice; freedom and peace. Read Singleton, "The Pattern at the Center" in Brandeis.
    Bring questions and your chart of purgatory for group discussion.

10 Quiz on purgatory.
    Guest lecture: S. Mary Brian Durkin on Dorothy Sayers' work on Dante. Prepare excerpt from Sayers on reserve.
    Exercise on purgatory due. Write a very brief analysis (3 pages typed) of one short section of the *Purgatorio* as allegory. Choose a few pages (1 to 3) of the text, summarize the action briefly (1 to 3 paragraphs), and then discuss what that action suggests to you about a person's inner life or about modern social life. If Dante's purgatory is a prescription or map for a happy life, what does your section prescribe allegorically? Be very strict in basing every conclusion you draw upon the poem itself.
    Introduction to paradise.

Part III: Fullness of Life
11   *Par.* I–V. 87: fidelity and failing; the moon.
     Par. V. 88–IX: men and women of the world, and lovers;
     Mercury and Venus.
     Music of the *Divine Comedy:* lecture-recital by S. Baptist Stohrer,
     O.P.
     Hand in initial outline for paper. See instructions below.
12   *Par.* X–XIV. 78: students and teachers; the sun. Have a conference
     this week on your paper topic and bibliography.
     Lecture on images in the *Paradiso,* parallels in the three canticles,
     Easter in the *Divine Comedy.* Hand in your revised and com-
     pleted outline and initial bibliography for your paper.
     Happy Easter! If you can, observe carefully the pageantry and
     symbolism of Catholic or Orthodox Holy Week services. Espe-
     cially try to observe the Easter Vigil service late Saturday night
     with its symbolism of light, fire, water, birth, night, freedom.
13   *Par.* XIV. 79–XVIII. 51: soldiers, family ties; Mars.
     Par. XVIII. 52–XXIII: rulers and world powers; Jove.
     Par. XXIV–XXIX: Dante's final examination in the heaven of the
     fixed stars and heaven itself. A backward look.
14   Field trip to planetarium.
     Dante's language. Readings from the *Divine Comedy* in Italian.
     Read the essays in Part I of Brandeis to help you understand
     Dante's reputation and influence.
     Par. XXX–XXXIII: the people of God and the vision of God in
     glory.
15   Review. Bring one or two questions and your chart of paradise.
     Papers due (3 copies). Discussion of examination questions and
     papers.
     Read others' papers as assigned and according to your interests.
     Discussion of papers.
16   Final examination.

Assignment for Final Paper

Write a brief research paper (5 to 8 pages typed) to help you review
the *Divine Comedy* and to get an idea of the critical literature about
Dante. The topic should be strictly limited, and the outline and draft
should be written from your study of the text; then you should read at
least the important works (books and articles and notes) on your subject and incorporate comments by and about these works into your
paper where appropriate, so that the reader can tell where your work

fits into the context of Dante studies, by agreement or disagreement, confirmation or addition. We hope that some of your essays will be suitable as entries in the annual competition of the Dante Society of America.

Possible topics:
The friendship of Dante and Vergil
The salvation of "pagans"
Male-female relations
Florence (or another city) in the *Divine Comedy*
Uses of one symbol in an episode
Allegory of one episode
Practical applications of Dante today (a single aspect)

TEACHING DANTE TO UNDERGRADUATES
AT PRINCETON

Robert Hollander

In the seven-hundredth anniversary of Dante's birth in 1965, three members of the Princeton faculty, graduates of Harvard, Yale, and Princeton, met periodically to discuss and shape two new courses to be offered in the section of European Literature of the Department of Romance Languages at Princeton University. The Harvard graduate, Edward Sullivan (who was shortly to become Dean of the College and who now, as Avalon Professor, serves as chairman of Princeton's Council of the Humanities), was then chairman of the department. The Yale graduate was A. Bartlett Giamatti, now president of Yale. I was the Princeton graduate.

The result of those deliberations was to dismantle the course that I had been giving since I came to Princeton in 1962, Masterworks of European Literature: *The Divine Comedy, Don Quixote, Faust*, and to redistribute the masterworks. *Faust*, a prodigal returned, was to go back over the border to the German Department; *Don Quixote* was to become a central text in one of the two new courses, Reason and Folly (readings from Erasmus to Dostoevsky); and Dante's poem was to become the sole object of study in a separate course. The Yale graduate, who was, as was I, a young assistant professor, was scheduled to give the course on Dante, which he had helped to design, while I was slated for Reason and Folly. My colleague never had the chance to give the Dante course, however, for Yale called him back that spring. As his legacy I received responsibility for giving not only Reason and Folly but the Dante course as well. That is a considerable debt to owe Bart Giamatti and Ed Sullivan.

Each year since 1967 (with time off for good behavior) I have offered Romance Languages and Literatures 303. Enrollments have varied from fifteen to fifty and in recent years seem to have leveled off at about twenty-five to thirty. The year that there were fifty students in the course (1969), which coincided with the most virulent phase of the supposed "greening" of America, was the year in which I decided, spurred by a large number of lax final examination papers, to put some teeth into the examination in the course. Thereafter students were given, in the first class meeting, some forty legal-size mimeographed sheets containing two hundred passages or "items" from the *Divine Comedy*. These remain the sole basis for both the midterm and the final examinations. In both these exercises students are asked to identify each item and its immediate context in the poem and to discuss the relation of that particular piece of Dante's poem to larger themes and motifs in the *Divine Comedy*. On the one-hour midterm students are confronted by ten items and on the three-hour final, where responses are expected to be more full, fifteen (mercifully down from an earlier twenty). This examination procedure is guaranteed to teach a willing student a good deal about the *Divine Comedy*. As unforgiving and demanding as this practice is, hardly any students have complained that it is excessive or that it forecloses on better options for study. (One year a waggish student's course evaluation rated the examinations "excellent," Dante himself only "very good.") The students who elect the course seem to know what they are getting into (a continuing campus tag has it that RLL 303 is the "organic chemistry of the humanities"). They come prepared to work. Walter Ong suggested in a lecture here in May of 1979 that, in monastic education, the learning of Latin was inextricably bound to the administration of corporal punishment. While the Dante course has no physical counterpart to such behavior, it does perhaps smack of a certain pained sodality. To say that one is enrolled in the Dante course conveys perhaps some intellectual distinction, but more a willingness to suffer, if in good company. Each September, when I look into the faces of those present at the first lecture, I wonder at the amount of labor to which each student is committed. At times I have recriminations about the amount of work that the course demands. The results of that labor, which become evident some four months later, more than reward the effort.

As for the pedagogical structure of the course, it becomes more informal as the term progresses. The first three weeks are devoted entirely to lectures (three hours). From then on we have one lecture a week (1½ hours), itself progressing somewhat more toward the discursive condition of a seminar as the term goes on, and one discussion with each smaller group (no more than ten) into which the class is divided. I also schedule a "Dante office hour," which is time made available only to *dantisti* in need of assistance or who simply desire to converse about the poem. During the first three weeks the students read the entire poem through once quickly. Thereafter we concentrate on particular cantos (see syllabus). Lectures during the first three weeks are dedicated to general introduction to the poem as literature, and attempt to give some sense of Dante's central matter and techniques. A major theme of these lectures is poetry's relation to truth, at least as I perceive Dante to have faced this essential question. Thus two of the six lectures are devoted to the question of allegory. Once we are all rereaders of the *Divine Comedy*, a poem that more than most cannot be read until one has read it, we stay very close to the text. Such critical activity, as everyone knows, is difficult, time-consuming, and tends to be disorganized. As I prepare to give the two "canned" lectures in the course, I often wish that I had the rest of the course on file cards too (I hasten to add that not even these lectures are *read* at the students). I resist that temptation on, I believe, sound grounds. Thus the course changes a good deal each year, reflecting both the interests of a particular group of students and my own developing interests. I should add that reading the *Vita nuova* seems to be of mixed value to the students. Reading it where we do (before entering the Earthly Paradise) works extremely well for those who are not put off by it; however, quite a few *are* put off by the work. On balance, it stays.

In addition to writing the two examinations, each student must present a paper of three to five thousand words after consulting with me about possible topics. Since the final examination is given before the Christmas vacation, students have about a month at their disposal for this assignment. Coming to the paper from the examinations, students frequently write papers that are impressive in their management of the details of the poem. In fact, in recent years four alumnae of the course have been winners in the annual contest for the best undergraduate paper on Dante sponsored by the Dante Society of America.

Although the course is given in English, we use a facing translation (Sinclair's or Singleton's) and the examinations are also bilingual. Thus students with Italian are able to do all or some (which is more frequently the case) of their work in the mother tongue. When there are enough Italian speakers, we form an Italian preceptorial, though even in that ambience most years conversation has been in English. While Cervantes is of course correct when he compares the reading of a work in translation to viewing a tapestry from the wrong side, a work like Dante's (or Cervantes') has so much in the way of narrative design and structure that the absence of texture can be, if not overlooked, at least not deplored totally.

It is difficult to write of one's own course in this way without the fear of self-puffery. And of course I am not able to see what I do not do as well as I should. All I can say is that I enjoy giving the course, am proud of it and of the students who take it. Many of them are continuing acquaintances, some have become friends. Blushing a little, I confess that, during Princeton's annual reunion weekend, we have for four years now held a "Dante reunion"; there is no sign that we shall cease. Those who care to spend an hour or so discussing a text in the poem and then somewhat more than that having drinks together. Writing this, I am aware how pleased I sound with this course. I cannot imagine my life without it.

COURSE SYLLABUS

WEEK		*Relevant handouts*
1	1. Organization; introduction	Plot Summary of *Aeneid;* Dante's Politics
	2. Introduction (continued)	Monsters and Rivers; Unity of the Moral Order of *Comedy*
2	3. The pattern of purgation (introduction to *Purgatory*)	Moore's Structure of Purgation
	4. Allegory I: history and theory	The Allegory of Dante's *Commedia*
3	5. Allegory II: Dante's practice	The Allegory of Dante's *Commedia*
	6. The geography of the ineffable (*Paradiso*)	The Geography of the Ineffable; The Invocations
4	7. *Inf.* I and II: introduction and epitome	a gloss on *alto ingegno*

	8. *Inf.* III–V: Dante's infernal population	*Inferno:* exemplars, and pity and fear
5	9. *Inf.* X, XIII, XV: the sympathetic sinners	
	10. *Inf.* XX, XXVI, XXXIII: the sympathetic sinners	
6	11. *Inf.* XXXIV, *Purg.* I–II: the pilgrims and Cato	*Convivo* IV. xxvi
	12. MIDTERM EXAMINATION (10 items)	
7	MIDTERM RECESS	
8	13. *Purg.* III–VI: the spirit of antepurgatory	
	14. *Purg.* XX. 124–XXII: Statius	
9	15. *Purg.* IX, XIX, XXVII: the dreams	
	16. *Purg.* XXIV–XXVI: on poetry and poets	
10	17. *Vita nuova*	
11	18. *Purg.* XXVIII–XXX: Matelda and Beatrice	
	19. *Purg.* XXX–XXXIII; *Inf.* I. 94–111: Beatrice and prophecy	
12	20. Left available for inevitable catching up with ourselves	
	21. *Paradiso:* epistemology and empire (*Par.* I. 67–72; II. 1–18; IV. 28–48; XXIII. 28–96; VI. 57–96; XVII. 70–96; XXVII. 139–48; XXX. 133–38)	
13	22. *Paradiso:* the language of Adam (*Par.* XIV. 76–96; XV. 25–48; XVI. 31–33; XVII. 31–35; XXVI. 109–38)	
	23. *Par.* XXV. 1–12; XXX–XXXIII: the ultimate vision	

TEACHING DANTE'S *DIVINE COMEDY* IN TRANSLATION

Amilcare A. Iannucci

Beginnings are important; hence, I begin my course on medieval Italian literature in translation, which is designed for third-year students but is also open to those in the second and fourth years, with an anecdote that plunges them immediately into Dante's world and casts them as interpreters. It also serves as a *captatio benevolentiae,* and as a point around which to fashion a discussion of the objectives of the course and of some of the problems we as modern readers of Dante face. The anecdote is recounted by Boccaccio in his *Life of Dante:*

> [Dante's] complexion was dark, and his hair and beard thick, black, and crisp; and his countenance always sad and thoughtful. And thus it happened one day in Verona . . . that, as he passed before a doorway where several women were sitting, one of them said to the others . . . "Do you see the man who goes down into hell and returns when he pleases, and brings back news of those who are below?" To which one of the others naïvely answered, "Indeed, what you say must be true; don't you see how his beard is crisped and his color darkened by the heat and smoke down there?"

153

Frivolous as it may seem, this little story tells us much about the nature of Dante's poem and its public.

Dante's *Divine Comedy*, like Boccaccio's own *Decameron*, was in its time what we would call an instant best-seller. The literate read, transcribed, and passed it on to friends—the manuscript tradition assures us of this. Those unable to read gathered eagerly in public squares to hear the latest news from the otherworld. Most, like the women of Verona, listened only for plot. Moreover, so powerful was their belief in the actual, physical existence of hell, and so persuasive were Dante's words in conjuring up that world, that they ingenuously mistook fiction for fact. But Boccaccio tells us that Dante, overhearing the women of Verona, was not unpleased with their reaction because it demonstrated that his "poema sacro" had provoked the desired effect. By perceiving Dante's words as literal, historical truth, the women of Verona had accepted the poem's ethical and didactic message, which is "to remove the living from the state of misery in this life and to guide them to a state of happiness," as the letter to Can Grande indicates.

Although the poem gives a surface appearance of simplicity, its meaning is, to use Dante's own term, "polysemous." Built into the poem's allegorical structure are a number of possible readings, all of which flow naturally from the literal narrative. It soon becomes apparent that in order to grasp the poem's complex structure of meaning and to appreciate its "hidden" beauties, mediation is necessary, not only for the women of Verona but for more sophisticated readers as well. So, shortly after Dante's death in 1321 the scholars went to work. Every verse was thoroughly glossed. By the end of the fourteenth century Dante's *Divine Comedy* had generated more commentary than Vergil's *Aeneid* had throughout the whole of the Middle Ages. Early on, therefore, the *Divine Comedy* was elevated from the rank of a best-seller to that of a classic, if one measure of a classic is the amount of criticism it has inspired.

Despite the sensational, even scandalous qualities of Dante's literal story that render his work accessible to all, the *Divine Comedy* is a difficult and profoundly ambiguous poem whose meaning is elusive; it thus demands constant reinterpretation and reevaluation. Does that mean that we have to endure it as a classic instead of enjoying it as a best-seller? Obviously, we, as sophisticated readers, cannot respond to the poem as the women of Verona did: immediately, uncritically, affectively. Too much water has passed under the Ponte Vecchio for that. But our reading of the poem risks being no less naïve than theirs unless we make an effort to establish an authentic dialogue with Dante and his world. The problem is one of distance: six centuries divide us from Dante. We no longer read the same books, share the same cultural assumptions, or hold the same world view as Dante and his contemporaries. Mythological, historical, and even geographical allusions are often lost on twentieth-century readers. To prevent an approximate, impressionistic reading of the poem, we must be prepared to fill in these gaps.

There is another barrier between the students and Dante in this course: language. We read the *Divine Comedy* in translation, and no matter how good the translation is, it can never be Dante. No translator can hope to capture the flow and rhythm of Dante's verse, simply because of the intrinsic differences between English and Italian. There is another hazard in translation. In the original text there are always ambiguities that the translator cannot reproduce. Before a difficult passage, he or she is obliged to adopt a critical stance. Thus, any translation of the *Divine Comedy* is heavily colored by the translator's interpretation of it. Interpretive options that exist in Dante's Italian are eliminated, and ambiguities, perhaps unknown to the original, are created. Not even prose translations can escape this kind of distortion. Indeed, they perpetrate another, more pervasive form of distortion: in their effort to secure the letter, they completely destroy the spirit. That is why I prefer a verse translation. In my opinion, it is worth sacrificing a little accuracy for a sense of Dante's poetry. Although it is not without shortcomings, I use Dorothy Sayers' translation of the *Divine Comedy*.

The *Divine Comedy*, then, needs mediation, now more than ever, if we are to avoid a simplistic, anachronistic reading. Since the poem's significance is polysemous, I strongly believe that we should apply to it all the critical instruments at our disposal rather than restrict ourselves to a single approach. Thus, the objective of this course is twofold: first, to help the students comprehend Dante's poetic world in the context of medieval culture and, second, to make them aware of the critical process itself. To this end, I have set up the course in the following manner:

1. A series of ten introductory lectures designed to bridge the historical and cultural gaps between us and Dante and to establish a critical framework within which to interpret the poem
2. Seminar reports by students based on key episodes from each of the three canticles
3. An introductory and concluding lecture on the *Purgatorio* and the *Paradiso*

The first two lectures reconstruct rapidly the genesis of the *Divine Comedy*. The first, woven around the figure of Beatrice, focuses on the poetic, spiritual, and intellectual evolution of Dante from the *Vita nuova* through the *Convivio* to the *Divine Comedy*. The second chronicles the political events that led to Dante's exile from Florence and explores the political, intellectual, and creative repercussions that experience had on Dante. I have discovered that a great deal of background material can be covered quickly and effectively by organizing the lectures in this manner around Beatrice and exile.

In the next three lectures I broach the problem of the poem's overall structure. What are the elements that give the *Divine Comedy* its form and unity? How do these elements reflect the thoughts and beliefs of Dante's world? For example, the stage on which Dante's "comedy" unfolds is the universe as it was conceived in his day. Thus, one of the most important elements of external structure is the Ptolemaic universe. Other elements that impose form on Dante's poem include the Thomistic-Aristotelian classification of sins and numerological symbolism. Before proceeding to an analysis of the poem's internal or allegorical structure, I review the allegorical problem in Dante in the light of the latest literature on the subject. But Dante's two major theoretical pronouncements on allegory (*Convivio* II. 1 and the letter to Can Grande, sections 7 and 8) provide the focus for the lecture. What is the difference between the "allegory of poets" and the "allegory of theologians"? What kind of allegory does Dante use in the *Divine Comedy?* Modern critical opinion, at least in North America, decrees that Dante's major, if not exclusive, mode of signifying in the *Divine Comedy* is the "allegory of theologians." If this is so, then how does Dante adapt the procedure to articulate the poem's two subjects: the pilgrim's journey through the three realms of the afterlife and the "state of souls after death"? After dealing with these questions of structure, I start to analyze the text.

I spend two classes on the prologue scene (*Inf.* I and II), going through it four times, each time viewing it from a different perspective. First, I simply explicate the literal sense. Then I consider it in terms of the pilgrim's personal history. But already in the prologue Dante the pilgrim is more than a figure of the historical Dante: he represents all of humanity. How does Dante the poet go about universalizing the pilgrim? In what way is the prologue a kind of mini–*Divine Comedy*, which, like the whole, is patterned on the dramatic unfolding of Christian history? Finally, I discuss the moral level of Dante's allegory. In the prologue Dante the poet sets up the metaphoric context for a moral interpretation of the poem. If the poem is to have a transforming effect, the reader too must take a journey, not a real journey into the world beyond, but one that is acted out in this life.

I use *Inferno* III to exemplify a close reading of the text in the tradition of the *lectura Dantis*. I analyze the canto verse by verse, making comments from stylistic, thematic, historical, theological, and other points of view. *Inferno* IV, on the other hand, poses certain critical problems that can best be dealt with from a historical point of view. The questions to ask here are: How and why does Dante depart from both the traditional theological and popular "poetic" representation of limbo?

The final lecture in the series returns to the problem of structure, this time at the level of the episode. Are there elements common to all the episodes in a given canticle? What are the essential elements that Dante uses to build the episode in the *Inferno?* Canto V, the first episode in hell proper, serves as the example. But there is more: How does Dante vary the pattern from episode to episode in order to make each seem new? In what way does the structure of the episode change from canticle to canticle? This last question I examine in more detail when I introduce the *Purgatorio* and the *Paradiso*.

To round off the students' knowledge of the historical and cultural context from which Dante's poem arose, I urge them to attend lectures and special videotape screenings organized by the Undergraduate Programme in Mediaeval Studies at St. Michael's College, University of Toronto, of which my course is a part. The lectures, given by prominent medievalists at the university from various disciplines (literature, philosophy, history, fine arts, music, etc.), include the following:

Grammar in the Trivium and the Language Arts
The Art of Memory and Its Roots in Rhetoric
Music as a Liberal Art
Handwritings and Handwritten Books in Common Use
The Autun Doorway (Last Judgment): Views of Life and Death
Boethius' *Consolation of Philosophy* and Dante's *Convivio*
Illuminated Manuscripts of the *Divine Comedy*

The videotapes (produced by the Centre for Mediaeval Studies at the University of Toronto) that I recommend are these:

The Planets
The Stars
The Making of a Manuscript

To Syngen and to Playe
The Fifteen Joys of Marriage
Le Roman de la Rose
King Arthur
The Crowning of Charlemagne
The Gothic Cathedral
The Last Judgment in Sculpture

Although most of these subjects do not deal with the *Divine Comedy* directly, they touch on issues and problems common to Dante and hence reinforce my lectures. Moreover, they often spark questions that lead to further discussion and development of issues in Dante. Since these activities are not a formal part of the course, they are not mandatory. Nonetheless, most of my students attend them.

Seminars are an essential part of the course and constitute about half of the course time during the term (two hours a week for fourteen weeks). They are important, I feel, because the traditional teacher-student relation in the classroom is broken down. Students are placed in the position of teachers and thus forced to acquire sufficient control over the material of the seminar to present it to their peers, to handle questions about it, and, if necessary, to defend their views. It is, of course, impossible to study the whole *Divine Comedy* in class, so the seminars focus on a few key episodes in each of the three canticles. But I stress to the students the importance of reading the poem chronologically, or canto by canto. The *Divine Comedy* is a work that reveals its meaning gradually and explicates itself as it unfolds.

The seminars conform to a particular format that I have found to be effective. Before students begin work on their topics, I ask them to consult me. The seminar, I explain, should be no more than twenty-five minutes, and if possible they should work from notes rather than read from a prepared text. Moreover, they must assume the responsibility of leading the discussion provoked by their papers. I instruct the other students to come to class armed with questions. I myself try to intervene in the discussion as little as possible, but I do reserve about five minutes at the end to tie loose ends and summarize. Students then have a week to write up the seminar in essay form, taking into account any points raised in class that seem significant. In assigning grades, I take into consideration both students' performance in class and the final written version of the seminar.

The whole exercise is worth fifty percent of the final grade. The rest of the grade is based on a one-hour test at the end of the term. Of the three questions on the test, the students must answer two, one as completely as possible in essay form, the other in outline form. Although the questions are general in scope, I require the students to answer them by making specific reference to at least two or three episodes in the poem. Here are two examples from past exams:

Discuss the changing relation between the literal and anagogical levels of Dante's allegory in the three canticles, using an episode from each canticle.

Discuss the various forms Dante's self-exegesis takes in the *Divine Comedy*, making specific references to the text.

The *Divine Comedy* is a work of education, and Dante as a poet-teacher wanted his poem to have a transforming effect on his readers. That is one of the principal functions of education. We as teachers of Dante use his poem to try to provoke a similar experience in our students. This can be exciting. Although we can no longer read Dante's poem as a best-seller and respond as immediately to its moral lesson as the women of Verona did, we can still enjoy it.

PARTICIPANTS IN SURVEY OF DANTE INSTRUCTORS

The generous and perceptive insights provided by these respondents to the Modern Language Association's request for information on teaching Dante have contributed significantly to the creation of this volume.

John B. Alphonso-Karkala
New York State University College, New Paltz

Mario Aste
University of Lowell

Kenneth Atchity
Occidental College

Grazia Avitabile
Wellesley College

Jean-Pierre Barricelli
University of California, Riverside

Albert Bonadeo
University of California, Santa Barbara

Emerson Brown, Jr.
Vanderbilt University

Mitzi M. Brunsdale
Mayville State College

Glauco Cambon
University of Connecticut

Ruth A. Cameron
Eastern Nazarene College

D. Allen Carroll
University of Tennessee, Knoxville

Mary J. Carruthers
University of Illinois, Chicago Circle

Anthony K. Cassell
University of Tennessee, Knoxville

Gaetano Cipolla
St. John's University

Kay J. Cosgrove
Hillsdale College

James G. Czarnecki
New York State University College, Potsdam

Sister Mary Clemente Davlin
Rosary College

Jeanne Dillon
Brown University

A. Dunlop
Auburn University

George D. Economou
Long Island University

Alfred Garvin Engstrom
University of North Carolina, Chapel Hill

Benedetto Fabrizi
Northeastern University

Giuseppe Faustini
Middlebury College

Wallace Fowlie
Duke University

Margherita Frankel
New York University

Philip Joseph Gallagher
University of Texas, El Paso

Stephen J. Gendzier
Brandeis University

Marie Giuriceo
Brooklyn College, City University of
  New York

Theodora R. Graham
Pennsylvania State University

Harlan Hamilton
Jersey City State College

John B. Harcourt
Ithaca College

Dabney Hart
Georgia State University

Sharon Harwood
Memphis State University

Elizabeth R. Hatcher
Towson State University

Emmanuel Hatzantonis
University of Oregon

Denise Heilbronn
Northern Illinois University

Robert Hollander
Princeton University

Julia Bolton Holloway
Princeton University

Kathryn L. S. Hutchinson
Georgia State University

Amilcare A. Iannucci
University of Toronto

Nicolae Iliescu
Harvard University

Rachel Jacoff
Wellesley College

James G. Jaroe
Hillsdale College

C. A. L. Jarrott
Loyola University

H. James Jensen
Indiana University

James B. King
Hillsdale College

Victoria Kirkham
University of Pennsylvania

Christopher Kleinhenz
University of Wisconsin, Madison

Judith J. Kollmann
University of Michigan, Flint

Richard H. Lansing
Brandeis University

Paul A. Lister
Sul Ross State University

William W. Main
University of Redlands

W. A. N. Mark
Niagara University

Ferdinando D. Maurino
University of Tennessee, Knoxville

David Mead
Georgia College

Marguerite P. Murphy
Manhattanville College

Mark Musa
Indiana University

Alan F. Nagel
University of Iowa

Lea (Bertani Vozar) Newman
North Adams State University

Hannibal S. Noce
University of Toronto

James C. Nohrnberg
University of Virginia

George R. Oetgen
Hillsdale College

R. Barton Palmer
Georgia State University

Anne Paolucci
St. John's University

Brooke Peirce
Goucher College

Roger J. Porter
Reed College

Joy Hambuechen Potter
University of Texas, Austin

Genevieve Quigley
Hillsdale College

Ricardo J. Quinones
Claremont Men's College

Walter Reinsdorf
Columbia-Greene Community
College

Robert V. V. Rice, Jr.
Hillsdale College

Robert J. Rodini
University of Wisconsin, Madison

Vinio Rossi
Oberlin College

Charles C. Russell
University of Maryland

Rinaldina Russell
Queens College, City University of
New York

Marilyn Schneider
University of Minnesota

Roberta Simone
Grand Valley State College

Eugenia M. Slavov
University of Delaware

Malinda Snow
Georgia State University

William A. Stephany
University of Vermont

Wesley D. Sweetser
New York State University College,
Oswego

Derek Traversi
Swarthmore College

Michael Ukas
University of Toronto

Martha S. Waller
Butler University

Barry Wood
University of Houston

WORKS CITED

Arthos, John. *Dante, Michelangelo, and Milton.* London: Routledge and Kegan Paul, 1963.

Asín Palacios, Miguel. *Islam and the* Divine Comedy. Trans. and ed. Harold Sutherland. 1926; rpt. New York: Barnes and Noble, 1968.

Associazione Italiana Editori. *Catalogo dei libri italiani in commercio.* Milan: Associazione Italiana Editori, 1970.

Auerbach, Erich. *Dante, Poet of the Secular World.* Trans. Ralph Manheim. Chicago: Univ. of Chicago Press, 1961.

———. *Literary Language and Its Public in Late Latin Antiquity and in the Middle Ages.* Trans. Ralph Manheim. New York: Pantheon, 1965.

Barbi, Michele. *Life of Dante.* Trans. and ed. Paul Ruggiers. Berkeley: Univ. of California Press, 1954.

Baron, Hans. *The Crisis in the Early Italian Renaissance: Civic Humanism and Republican Liberty in an Age of Classicism and Tyranny.* 1955; rpt. Princeton: Princeton Univ. Press, 1966.

Bergin, Thomas G. *Dante.* New York: Orion, 1965.

———. *A Diversity of Dante.* New Brunswick, N.J.: Rutgers Univ. Press, 1969.

———. *Perspectives on the* Divine Comedy. Bloomington: Indiana Univ. Press, 1970.

———, trans. *The Divine Comedy.* New York: Appleton-Century-Crofts, 1954.

———, trans. *The Divine Comedy.* Illus. Leonard Baskin. 3 vols. New York: Grossman, 1969.

———, ed. *From Time to Eternity: Essays on Dante's* Divine Comedy. New Haven: Yale Univ. Press, 1967.

Biancolli, Louis. *The Divine Comedy.* Illus. Harry Bennett. New York: Washington Square Press, 1969.

Bigongiari, Dino. *Essays on Dante and Medieval Culture: Critical Studies of the Thought and Texts of Dante, St. Augustine, St. Thomas Aquinas, Marsilius of Padua, and Other Medieval Subjects.* Introd. Henry Paolucci. Florence: Olschki, 1964.

Blake, William. *Illustrations to the* Divine Comedy. 1922; rpt. New York: Da Capo Press, 1968.

Block, Haskell, ed. *The Teaching of World Literature: Proceedings of the Conference on the Teaching of World Literature, University of Wisconsin, 1959.* Chapel Hill: Univ. of North Carolina Press, 1960.

Boccaccio, Giovanni, and Leonardo Bruni Aretino. *The Earliest Lives of Dante.* Trans. James Robinson Smith. 1901; rpt. New York: Ungar, 1963.

Botticelli, Sandro. *The Drawings by Sandro Botticelli for Dante's* Divine Comedy. Ed. and introd. Kenneth Clark. New York: Harper, 1976.

Bottiglia, William F. "Dante at M.I.T.: A New Pedagogical Approach." *Italica*, 42 (1965), 184–90.

Boyde, Patrick. *Dante's Style in His Lyric Poetry.* Cambridge: Cambridge Univ. Press, 1971.

Branca, Vittore, and Ettore Caccia, eds. *Dante nel mondo.* Florence: Olschki, 1965.

Brandeis, Irma. *The Ladder of Vision: A Study of Dante's* Comedy. Garden City, N.Y.: Doubleday, 1960.

———, ed. *Discussions of the* Divine Comedy. Boston: Heath, 1961.

Brieger, Peter, Millard Meiss, and Charles S. Singleton. *Illuminated Manuscripts of the* Divine Comedy. 2 vols. Bollingen Series, 81. Princeton: Princeton Univ. Press, 1969.

Cali, Pietro. *Allegory and Vision in Dante and Langland.* Cork: Cork Univ. Press, 1971.

Cambon, Glauco. *Dante's Craft: Studies in Language and Style.* Minneapolis: Univ. of Minnesota Press, 1969.

Carlyle, John Aitken, Thomas Okey, and Philip Henry Wicksteed, trans. *The Divine Comedy.* New York: Vintage, n.d.

Casini, Tommaso, and S. A. Barbi, eds. *La divina commedia di Dante Alighieri.* 6th ed. Florence: Sansoni, 1921.

Chandler, S. Bernard, and J. A. Molinaro. *The World of Dante: Six Studies in Language and Thought.* Toronto: Univ. of Toronto Press, 1966.

Charity, Alan Clifford. *Events and Their Afterlife: The Dialectics of Christian Typology in the Bible and Dante.* Cambridge: Cambridge Univ. Press, 1966.

Chaytor, Henry John. *The Troubadours of Dante: Selections from the Works of the Provençal Poets Quoted by Dante.* 1892; rpt. New York: AMS, 1974.

Chubb, Thomas Caldecot. *Dante and His World.* Boston: Little, Brown, 1967.

Ciardi, John, trans. *The Inferno.* New York: New American Library, 1954.

———, trans. *The Purgatorio.* New York: New American Library, 1961.

———, trans. *The Paradiso.* New York: New American Library, 1970.

Clements, Robert J., ed. *American Critical Essays on* The Divine Comedy. New York: New York Univ. Press, 1967.

Colish, Marcia L. *The Mirror of Language: A Study in the Medieval Theory of Knowledge.* New Haven: Yale Univ. Press, 1968.

Cook, Albert. *The Classical Line: A Study in Epic Poetry.* Bloomington: Indiana Univ. Press, 1967.

Cosmo, Umberto. *A Handbook to Dante Studies.* Trans. David Moore. Oxford: Blackwell, 1950.

Coulton, G. G. *Medieval Panorama: The English Scene from Conquest to Reformation.* 1938; rpt. New York: Noonday, 1955.

Croce, Benedetto. *The Poetry of Dante.* Trans. Douglas Ainslie. 1922; rpt. Mamaroneck, N.Y.: Appel, 1971.

Cunningham, Gilbert F. *The* Divine Comedy *in English: A Critical Bibliography.* 2 vols. Edinburgh: Oliver and Boyd, 1965–67.

Curtius, Ernst Robert. *European Literature and the Latin Middle Ages.* Trans. Willard R. Trask. 1953; rpt. New York: Harper, 1963.

Dante Society of America. *A Concordance to the* Divine Comedy. Ed. Ernest Hatch Wilkins and Thomas G. Bergin. Cambridge, Mass.: Harvard Univ. Press, 1966.

Davis, Charles Till. *Dante and the Idea of Rome.* Oxford: Clarendon, 1957.

Demaray, John G. *The Invention of Dante's* Commedia. New Haven: Yale Univ. Press, 1974.

De Sanctis, Francesco. *De Sanctis on Dante.* Ed. and trans. Joseph Rossi and Alfred Galpin. Madison: Univ. of Wisconsin Press, 1959.

DeSua, William J. *Dante into English: A Study of the Translation of the* Divine Comedy *in Britain and America.* Chapel Hill: Univ. of North Carolina Press, 1964.

———, and Gino Rizzo, eds. *A Dante Symposium.* Chapel Hill: Univ. of North Carolina Press, 1965.

Dinsmore, Charles Allen. *The Teachings of Dante.* Boston: Houghton Mifflin, 1901.

Dunbar, Helen Flanders. *Symbolism in Medieval Thought and Its Consummation in the* Divine Comedy. 1929; rpt. New York: Russell and Russell, 1961.

Eliot, T. S. *Dante.* London: Faber and Faber, 1929.

Enciclopedia dantesca. Ed. Umberto Bosco, Giorgio Petrocchi, et al. Rome: Istituto della Enciclopedia Italiana, 1970–76.

Enciclopedia italiana. Rome: Istituto della Enciclopedia Italiana, 1950.

Esposito, Enzo. *Gli studi danteschi dal 1950 al 1964.* Rome: Centro Editoriale Internazionale, 1965.

Fay, Edward Allen. *Concordance of the* Divina commedia. 2 vols. 1888; rpt. New York: Haskel House, 1969.

Fergusson, Francis. *Dante's Drama of the Mind: A Modern Reading of the* Purgatorio. Princeton: Princeton Univ. Press, 1953.

———. *Dante.* New York: Macmillan, 1966.

———. *Trope and Allegory: Themes Common to Dante and Shakespeare.* Athens: Univ. of Georgia Press, 1977.

Ferrante, Joan M. *Woman as Image in Medieval Literature: From the Twelfth Century to Dante*. New York: Columbia Univ. Press, 1975.

Foster, Kenelm, O.P. *The Two Dantes and Other Studies*. Berkeley: Univ. of California Press, 1977.

Fowlie, Wallace. *A Reading of Dante's* Inferno. Chicago: Univ. of Chicago Press, 1981.

Fox, Ruth Mary. *Dante Lights the Way*. Milwaukee, Wis.: Bruce, 1958.

Freccero, John, ed. *Dante: A Collection of Critical Essays*. Englewood Cliffs, N.J.: Prentice-Hall, 1965.

———. "The *Divine Comedy*." Cassette. Deland, Fla.: Everett/Edwards, n.d. [Lecture.]

Friederich, Werner P. *Dante's Fame Abroad, 1350–1850: The Influence of Dante Alighieri on the Poets and Scholars of Spain, France, England, Germany, Switzerland, and the U.S.* Chapel Hill: Univ. of North Carolina Press, 1950.

Gardner, Edmund Garratt. *Dante's Ten Heavens: A Study of the* Paradiso. 1898; rpt. New York: Haskell House, 1970.

———. *Dante and the Mystics: A Study of the Mystical Aspect of the* Divine Comedy *and Its Relations with Some of Its Mediaeval Sources*. New York: Dutton, 1913.

Giamatti, A. Bartlett. *The Earthly Paradise and the Renaissance Epic*. Princeton: Princeton Univ. Press, 1966.

Gilbert, Allan H. *Dante's Conception of Justice*. 1925; rpt. New York: AMS, 1965.

———. *Dante and His* Comedy. New York: New York Univ. Press, 1963.

Gilson, Etienne. *Dante and Philosophy*. Trans. David Moore. 1949; rpt. New York: Harper, 1963.

The Golden Age of the Madrigal. Vol. 7. New York: Schirmer, 1942.

Grandgent, Charles H. *Companion to the* Divine Comedy. Ed. Charles S. Singleton. Cambridge, Mass.: Harvard Univ. Press, 1975.

———, ed. *La divina commedia*. Rev. Charles S. Singleton. Cambridge, Mass.: Harvard Univ. Press, 1972.

Gurteen, S. Humphries. *The Epic of the Fall of Man: A Comparative Study of Caedmon, Dante, and Milton*. 1896; rpt. New York: Haskell House, 1964.

Highet, Gilbert. *The Classical Tradition: Greek and Roman Influences on Western Literature*. New York: Oxford Univ. Press, 1957.

Holbrook, Richard Thayer. *Dante and the Animal Kingdom*. 1902; rpt. New York: AMS, 1966.

———. *Portraits of Dante from Giotto to Raffael: A Critical Study*. Boston: Houghton Mifflin, 1911.

Hollander, Robert. *Allegory in Dante's* Commedia. Princeton. Princeton Univ. Press, 1969.

——, and A. Bartlett Giamatti, eds. *Western Literature II: The Middle Ages, Renaissance, Enlightenment.* New York: Harcourt, 1971.

Hopper, Vincent Forster. *Medieval Number Symbolism: Its Sources, Meaning, and Influence on Thought and Expression.* 1938; rpt. New York: Cooper Square, 1969.

Huse, H. R., trans. *The Divine Comedy.* New York: Holt, 1954.

Jackson, W. T. H. *Medieval Literature: A History and a Guide.* New York: Collier, 1966.

Kay, George, ed. *Penguin Book of Italian Verse.* Baltimore: Penguin, 1958.

Kirkpatrick, Robin. *Dante's* Paradiso *and the Limitations of Modern Criticism: A Study of Style and Poetic Theory.* Cambridge: Cambridge Univ. Press, 1975.

Kohler, Kaufman. *Heaven and Hell in Comparative Religion.* New York: Macmillan, 1923.

Kuhns, L. Oscar. *The Treatment of Nature in Dante's* Divina commedia. 1897; rpt. Port Washington, N.Y.: Kennikat, 1971.

Lagercrantz, Olaf Gustaf Hugo. *From Hell to Paradise: Dante and His* Comedy. Trans. Alan Blair. New York: Washington Square, 1966.

Lansing, Richard H. *From Image to Idea: A Study of the Simile in Dante's* Commedia. Ravenna: Longo, 1977.

LaPiana, Angelina. *Dante's American Pilgrimage: A Historical Survey of Dante Studies in the United States, 1800–1944.* New Haven: Yale Univ. Press, 1948.

Lebrun, Federico. *Drawings for Dante's* Inferno. n.p.: Kanthos Press, 1963.

Lewis, C. S. *The Allegory of Love: A Study in Medieval Tradition.* 1936; rpt. New York: Oxford Univ. Press, 1958.

——. *The Discarded Image: An Introduction to Medieval and Renaissance Literature.* Cambridge: Cambridge Univ. Press, 1964.

Lewis, Ewart. *Medieval Political Ideas.* 2 vols. New York: Knopf, 1954.

Limentani, Uberto, ed. *The Mind of Dante.* Cambridge: Cambridge Univ. Press, 1965.

Lovejoy, A. O. *The Great Chain of Being: A Study in the History of an Idea.* Cambridge, Mass.: Harvard Univ. Press, 1936.

Lovera, Luciano, Rosanna Bellarini, and Anna Mazzarello, eds. *Concordanza della* Commedia *di Dante Alighieri.* Turin: Einaudi, 1975.

Luke, Helen M. *Dark Wood to White Rose: A Study of Meanings in Dante's* Divine Comedy. Pecos, N.M.: Dove, 1975.

Mack, Maynard, et al., eds. *The Norton Anthology of World Masterpieces.* 2 vols. 4th ed. New York: Norton, 1980.

Mather, Frank Jewett. *The Portraits of Dante Compared with the Measurements of His Skull and Reclassified.* Princeton: Princeton Univ. Press, 1921.

Mazzeo, Joseph A. *Structure and Thought in the* Paradiso. Ithaca, N.Y.: Cornell Univ. Press, 1958.

———. *Medieval Cultural Tradition in Dante's* Comedy. Ithaca, N.Y.: Cornell Univ. Press, 1960.

Mazzotta, Giuseppe. *Dante, Poet of the Desert: History and Allegory in the* Divine Comedy. Princeton: Princeton Univ. Press, 1979.

Milano, Paolo, ed. *The Portable Dante.* New York: Viking, 1947.

Mineo, Nicolò. *Dante.* Bari: Laterza, 1971.

Montano, Rocco. *Storia della poesia di Dante.* 2 vols. Naples: Quaderni di Delta, 1962.

Montgomery, Marion. *The Reflective Journey toward Order: Essays on Dante, Wordsworth, Eliot, and Others.* Athens: Univ. of Georgia Press, 1973.

Musa, Mark. *Advent at the Gates: Dante's* Comedy. Bloomington: Indiana Univ. Press, 1974.

———, trans. *Dante's* Inferno. Bloomington: Indiana Univ. Press, 1971.

———, ed. *Essays on Dante.* Bloomington: Indiana Univ. Press, 1964.

Needler, Howard. *Saint Francis and Saint Dominic in the* Divine Comedy. Krefeld, West Germany: Scherpe, 1969.

Oliver, Kenneth. "Dante in a World Literature Course." *Yearbook of General and Comparative Literature,* 3 (1954), 46–51.

Olschki, Leonardo. *The Genius of Italy.* Ithaca, N.Y.: Cornell Univ. Press, 1954.

Orr, Mary A. *Dante and the Early Astronomers.* 1913; rpt., with Introd. by Barbara Reynolds, New York: Hillary House, 1961.

Padoan, Giorgio. *Introduzione a Dante.* Florence: Sansoni, 1975.

Paolucci, Anne. "Dante and Machiavelli." Cassette. Deland, Fla.: Everett/Edwards, n.d. [Lecture.]

Passerin d'Entrèves, Alessandro. *Dante as a Political Thinker.* Oxford: Clarendon, 1952.

Petrocchi, Giorgio. *La commedia secondo l'antica vulgata.* 4 vols. Milan: Mondadori, 1966–67.

Pipa, Arshi. *Montale and Dante.* Minneapolis: Univ. of Minnesota Press, 1968.

Pound, Ezra. *The Spirit of Romance.* New York: New Directions, 1968.

Praz, Mario. *The Flaming Heart: Essays on Crashaw, Machiavelli, and Other Studies in the Relations between Italian and English Literature from Chaucer to T. S. Eliot.* Garden City, N.Y.: Doubleday, 1958.

Quinones, Ricardo J. *The Renaissance Discovery of Time.* Cambridge, Mass.: Harvard Univ. Press, 1972.

———. *Dante Alighieri.* Boston: Twayne, 1979.

Ralphs, Sheila. *Etterno Spiro: A Study in the Nature of Dante's* Paradiso. New York: Barnes and Noble, 1962.

———. *Dante's Journey to the Center: Some Patterns in His Allegory.* New York: Barnes and Noble, 1973.

Rauschenberg, Robert. *Rauschenberg: Thirty-four Drawings for Dante's* Inferno. Comm. by Doré Ashton. New York: Abrams, 1964.

Reade, William H. V. *The Moral System of Dante's* Inferno. 1909; rpt. Port Washington, N.Y.: Kennikat, 1969.

Reynolds, Mary T. *Dante and Joyce: The Shaping Imagination.* Princeton: Princeton Univ. Press, 1981.

Roche, Jerome. *The Madrigal.* New York: Scribner, 1972.

Roe, Albert S., ed. *Blake's Illustrations to the* Divine Comedy. 1953; rpt., Westport, Conn.: Greenwood, 1977.

Rougement, Denis de. *Love in the Western World.* Trans. Montgomery Belgion. Rev. ed. New York: Pantheon, 1956.

Routh, Harold Victor. *God, Man, and Epic Poetry: A Study in Comparative Literature.* 2 vols. 1927; rpt. Westport, Conn.: Greenwood, 1969.

Ruggiers, Paul G. *Florence in the Age of Dante.* Norman: Univ. of Oklahoma Press, 1964.

Samuel, Irene. *Dante and Milton: The* Commedia *and* Paradise Lost. Ithaca, N.Y.: Cornell Univ. Press, 1966.

Santayana, George. *Three Philosophical Poets: Lucretius, Dante, and Goethe.* 1910; rpt. Cambridge, Mass.: Harvard Univ. Press, 1944.

Sapegno, Natalino, ed. *La divina commedia.* 3 vols. Rev. ed. Florence: La Nuova Italia, 1968.

Sayers, Dorothy L. *Introductory Papers on Dante.* New York: Harper, 1955.

———. *Further Papers on Dante.* New York: Harper, 1957.

———, trans. *Cantica I: Hell (L'Inferno).* Baltimore: Penguin, 1949.

———, trans. *Cantica II: Purgatory (Il Purgatorio).* Baltimore: Penguin, 1955.

———, and Barbara Reynolds, trans. *Cantica III: Paradise (Il Paradiso).* Baltimore: Penguin, 1962.

Scartazzini, Giovanni Andrea. *Enciclopedia dantesca: Dizionario critico e ragionato di quanto concerne la vita e le opere di Dante Alighieri.* Milan: Hoepli, 1896–1905.

Schettino, Franca, ed. *A Dante Profile.* Los Angeles: Univ. of Southern California Press, 1967.

Schevill, Ferdinand. *Medieval and Renaissance Florence.* 2 vols. New York: Harper Torchbooks, 1963.

Schless, Howard. *Dante and Chaucer.* Norman, Okla.: Pilgrim Books, 1981.

"A Selection from Dante's Iconography." *Italian Quarterly*, 9 (Spring 1965), center inset.

Sells, A. L. *The Italian Influence in English Poetry from Chaucer to Southwell*. Bloomington: Indiana Univ. Press, 1955.

Seward, Barbara. *The Symbolic Rose*. New York: Columbia Univ. Press, 1960.

Shapiro, Marianne. *Women, Earthly and Divine, in the* Comedy *of Dante*. Lexington: Univ. of Kentucky Press, 1975.

Siebzehner-Vivanti, Giorgio. *Dizionario della* Divina commedia. 1954; rpt. Milan: Feltrinelli, 1965.

Sinclair, John D., trans. *Dante's* Inferno. 1939; rpt. New York: Oxford Univ. Press, 1970.

———, trans. *Dante's* Purgatorio. 1939; rpt. New York: Oxford Univ. Press, 1970.

———, trans. *Dante's* Paradiso. 1946; rpt. New York: Oxford Univ. Press, 1970.

Singleton, Charles S. *An Essay on the* Vita nuova. Cambridge, Mass.: Harvard Univ. Press, 1949.

———. *Dante Studies 1.* Commedia: *Elements of Structure*. Cambridge, Mass.: Harvard Univ. Press, 1954.

———. *Dante Studies 2. Journey to Beatrice*. Cambridge, Mass.: Harvard Univ. Press, 1958.

———, trans. *The Divine Comedy*. 3 two-part vols. Princeton: Princeton Univ. Press, 1970–75.

———, trans. *Inferno: Text and Commentary*. 1970; rpt. Princeton: Princeton Univ. Press, 1980.

Spingarn, J. E. *A History of Literary Criticism in the Renaissance*. 2nd ed. 1908; rpt. New York: Harcourt, 1963.

Stambler, Bernard. *Dante's Other World: The* Purgatorio *as Guide to the Divine Comedy*. New York: New York Univ. Press, 1957.

Stanford, W. B. *The Ulysses Theme: A Study in the Adaptability of a Traditional Hero*. 2nd ed. New York: Barnes and Noble, 1964.

Swing, Thomas K. *The Fragile Leaves of the Sybil: Dante's Master Plan*. Westminster, Md.: Newman Press, 1962.

Sypher, Wylie. *Four Stages of Renaissance Style: Transformations in Art and Literature, 1400–1700*. Garden City, N.Y.: Doubleday, 1955.

Tate, Bill, ed. *Flaxman's Designs for Dante:* Inferno, Purgatorio, Paradiso. Truchas, N.M.: Tate Gallery, 1968.

Thompson, David. *Dante's Epic Journeys*. Baltimore: Johns Hopkins Univ. Press, 1974.

———, comp. *The Three Crowns of Florence: Humanistic Assessments of Dante, Petrarca, and Boccaccio*. Ed. and trans. David Thompson and Alan F. Nagel. New York: Harper, 1972.

Toynbee, Paget Jackson. *Dante in English Literature from Chaucer to Cary.* 2 vols. London: Methuen, 1909.

———. *Concise Dictionary of Proper Names and Notable Matters in the Works of Dante.* 1914; rpt. New York: Phaeton, 1968.

———. *A Dictionary of Proper Names and Notable Matters in the Works of Dante.* Rev. Charles S. Singleton. Oxford: Clarendon, 1968.

Valency, Maurice. *In Praise of Love: An Introduction to the Love Poetry of the Renaissance.* New York: Macmillan, 1958.

Vallone, Aldo. *Gli studi danteschi dal 1940 al 1949.* Florence: Olschki, 1950.

Vandelli, Giuseppe, ed. *Testo critico della* Divina commedia. Comm. by G. A. Scartazzini. Rev. ed. Milan: Hoepli, 1929.

Vittorini, Domenico. *The Age of Dante: A Concise History of Italian Culture in the Years of the Early Renaissance.* Illus. Fred Haucke. Syracuse, N.Y.: Syracuse Univ. Press, 1957.

Vossler, Karl. *Mediaeval Culture: An Introduction to Dante and His Times.* Trans. William Cranston Lawton. 2 vols. 1929; rpt. New York: Ungar, 1958.

Weinberg, Bernard. *A History of Literary Criticism in the Italian Renaissance.* 2 vols. Chicago: Univ. of Chicago Press, 1961.

White, Lawrence Grant, trans. *The Divine Comedy.* Illus. Gustave Doré. New York: Pantheon, 1948.

Wicksteed, Philip Henry. *Dante and Aquinas.* 1913; rpt. New York: Haskell House, 1971.

Wilhelm, James J. *Dante and Pound: The Epic of Judgement.* Orono: Univ. of Maine Press, 1974.

Wilkins, Ernest Hatch. *Dante: Poet and Apostle.* Chicago: Univ. of Chicago Press, 1921.

Williams, Charles. *The Figure of Beatrice: A Study in Dante.* 1943; rpt. New York: Noonday, 1961.

Wyld, M. Alice. *The Dread* Inferno: *Notes for Beginners in the Study of Dante.* 1904; rpt. Port Washington, N.Y.: Kennikat, 1961.

Yeats, W. B. *Essays and Introductions.* New York: Macmillan, 1961.

Zingarelli, Nicola. *La vita, i tempi, e le opere di Dante.* 2 vols. Milan: Vallardi, 1931.

INDEX

173

Modern Language Association of America
Approaches to Teaching World Literature
Joseph Gibaldi, series editor

Achebe's Things Fall Apart. Ed. Bernth Lindfors. 1991.
Arthurian Tradition. Ed. Maureen Fries and Jeanie Watson. 1992.
Austen's Pride and Prejudice. Ed. Marcia McClintock Folsom. 1993.
Beckett's Waiting for Godot. Ed. June Schlueter and Enoch Brater. 1991.
Beowulf. Ed. Jess B. Bessinger, Jr., and Robert F. Yeager. 1984.
Blake's Songs of Innocence and of Experience. Ed. Robert F. Gleckner and
 Mark L. Greenberg. 1989.
Brontë's Jane Eyre. Ed. Diane Long Hoeveler and Beth Lau. 1993.
Byron's Poetry. Ed. Frederick W. Shilstone. 1991.
Camus's The Plague. Ed. Steven G. Kellman. 1985.
Cather's My Ántonia. Ed. Susan J. Rosowski. 1989.
Cervantes' Don Quixote. Ed. Richard Bjornson. 1984.
Chaucer's Canterbury Tales. Ed. Joseph Gibaldi. 1980.
Chopin's The Awakening. Ed. Bernard Koloski. 1988.
Coleridge's Poetry and Prose. Ed. Richard E. Matlak. 1991.
Dante's Divine Comedy. Ed. Carole Slade. 1982.
Dickens' David Copperfield. Ed. Richard J. Dunn. 1984.
Dickinson's Poetry. Ed. Robin Riley Fast and Christine Mack Gordon. 1989.
Eliot's Middlemarch. Ed. Kathleen Blake. 1990.
Eliot's Poetry and Plays. Ed. Jewel Spears Brooker. 1988.
Ellison's Invisible Man. Ed. Susan Resneck Parr and Pancho Savery. 1989.
Flaubert's Madame Bovary. Ed. Laurence M. Porter and Eugene F. Gray. 1995.
García Márquez's One Hundred Years of Solitude. Ed. María Elena de Valdés and
 Mario J. Valdés. 1990.
Goethe's Faust. Ed. Douglas J. McMillan. 1987.
Hebrew Bible as Literature in Translation. Ed. Barry N. Olshen and
 Yael S. Feldman. 1989.
Homer's Iliad *and* Odyssey. Ed. Kostas Myrsiades. 1987.
Ibsen's A Doll House. Ed. Yvonne Shafer. 1985.
Works of Samuel Johnson. Ed. David R. Anderson and Gwin J. Kolb. 1993.
Joyce's Ulysses. Ed. Kathleen McCormick and Erwin R. Steinberg. 1993.
Kafka's Short Fiction. Ed. Richard T. Gray. 1995.
Keats's Poetry. Ed. Walter H. Evert and Jack W. Rhodes. 1991.
Kingston's The Woman Warrior. Ed. Shirley Geok-lin Lim. 1991.
Lessing's The Golden Notebook. Ed. Carey Kaplan and Ellen Cronan Rose. 1989.
Mann's Death in Venice *and Other Short Fiction*. Ed. Jeffrey B. Berlin. 1992.
Medieval English Drama. Ed. Richard K. Emmerson. 1990.
Melville's Moby-Dick. Ed. Martin Bickman. 1985.
Metaphysical Poets. Ed. Sidney Gottlieb. 1990.
Miller's Death of a Salesman. Ed. Matthew C. Roudané. 1995.
Milton's Paradise Lost. Ed. Galbraith M. Crump. 1986.

Molière's Tartuffe *and Other Plays*. Ed. James F. Gaines and
    Michael S. Koppisch. 1995.
Momaday's The Way to Rainy Mountain. Ed. Kenneth M. Roemer. 1988.
Montaigne's Essays. Ed. Patrick Henry. 1994.
Murasaki Shikibu's The Tale of Genji. Ed. Edward Kamens. 1993.
Pope's Poetry. Ed. Wallace Jackson and R. Paul Yoder. 1993.
Shakespeare's King Lear. Ed. Robert H. Ray. 1986.
Shakespeare's The Tempest *and Other Late Romances*. Ed. Maurice Hunt. 1992.
Shelley's Frankenstein. Ed. Stephen C. Behrendt. 1990.
Shelley's Poetry. Ed. Spencer Hall. 1990.
Sir Gawain and the Green Knight. Ed. Miriam Youngerman Miller and
    Jane Chance. 1986.
Spenser's Faerie Queene. Ed. David Lee Miller and Alexander Dunlop. 1994.
Sterne's Tristram Shandy. Ed. Melvyn New. 1989.
Swift's Gulliver's Travels. Ed. Edward J. Rielly. 1988.
Voltaire's Candide. Ed. Renée Waldinger. 1987.
Whitman's Leaves of Grass. Ed. Donald D. Kummings. 1990.
Wordsworth's Poetry. Ed. Spencer Hall, with Jonathan Ramsey. 1986.